Adulting and Life Skills

The Everything You Need to Know Guide for the Brand New Adult

Elizabeth Weston

© **Copyright 2024 - All rights reserved.**

The content contained within this book may not be reproduced, duplicated or transmitted without direct written permission from the author or the publisher.

Under no circumstances will any blame or legal responsibility be held against the publisher, or author, for any damages, reparation, or monetary loss due to the information contained within this book, either directly or indirectly.

Legal Notice:

This book is copyright protected. It is only for personal use. You cannot amend, distribute, sell, use, quote or paraphrase any part, or the content within this book, without the consent of the author or publisher.

Disclaimer Notice:

Please note the information contained within this document is for educational and entertainment purposes only. All effort has been executed to present accurate, up to date, reliable, complete information. No warranties of any kind are declared or implied. Readers acknowledge that the author is not engaged in the rendering of legal, financial, medical or professional advice. The content within this book has been derived from various sources. Please consult a licensed professional before attempting any techniques outlined in this book.

By reading this document, the reader agrees that under no circumstances is the author responsible for any losses, direct or indirect, that are incurred as a result of the use of the information contained within this document, including, but not limited to, errors, omissions, or inaccuracies.

Table of Contents

INTRODUCTION 1

CHAPTER 1: LIFE SKILLS & HABITS 5
   TIME MANAGEMENT & TIME ROBBERS 5
   HOUSEHOLD CHORES, UTILITIES, & HOW-TO'S 8
      Laundry 8
      Dishes 10
      Mini Chores/Minimum Maintenance 11
      Meal Planning 13
   UNDERSTANDING UTILITIES 14

CHAPTER 2: HOME REPAIR, DECOR, & SAFETY 17
   PLUMBING 17
      Toilets 18
      Faucets 18
      Drains 19
      Frozen Pipes & ACs 19
      Leaky Wall/Floor/Ceiling 20
   ELECTRICAL 20
      Light Fixtures 20
      Useless Light Switches 21
      Circuit breaker 21
      Warning signs 22
   HOME IMPROVEMENT 22
      Basic Tools 23
      Cabinets & Doors 23
      Pictures 24
      Curtains 24
      Shelves 25
   HEATING/COOLING 26
   APPLIANCES 27
      Fridge 27
      Dishwasher 27
      Oven 28
      Microwave 28
      Toaster/Toaster Oven 29
      Vacuum 29

SAFETY 29
    Smoke Detectors 30
    Fire Extinguishers & Blankets 30
    Security Systems 31

CHAPTER 3: HEALTH, WELLNESS, & FIRST AID 33

HYGIENE 33
NUTRITION 35
    Fast Food 36
    Cooking at Home 36
    Nutritional Evaluation of Each 37
    Cooking Tips 37
FITNESS 38
    Balancing Fitness With Busy Schedules 38
    Exercise Options 39
    Tips for Home Workouts 40
    Safety Precautions 40
MENTAL HEALTH 41
HEALTH INSURANCE 42
FIRST AID 43
    Basic First Aid Kit Necessities 43
    Cuts, Scrapes, & Bites 44
    Burns 44
    Allergic Reactions 45
    When To See a Doctor 46

CHAPTER 4: FINANCIAL LITERACY 47

CREDIT SCORE 47
BASIC BUDGETING SKILLS & MANAGING EXPENSES 48
    Savings 48
    Budget Plan 48
    Credit Cards 49
SCHOLARSHIPS & STUDENT LOANS 51
    Scholarships 51
    Student Loans 52
    Managing Debt After College 53

CHAPTER 5: TAXES & CIVIC KNOWLEDGE 55

PAYING TAXES 55
    Tax Filing 56
VOTING REGISTRATION 58
    Step 1: Know the Basics 58
    Step 2: Registering to Vote 58
    Step 3: Current Registration 59

  Step 4: Voting Options *59*
  Step 5: Get Informed *59*
 JURY DUTY *59*
  What is Jury Duty and How Do You Get Chosen? *59*
  What Happens After You Get Summoned?................................ *60*
  Is There a Way to Get Out of Jury Duty?.................................... *60*
  Other Things to Know *61*

CHAPTER 6: EMERGENCY PREPAREDNESS 65

 GO-BAG ESSENTIALS.. 65
 WEATHER-RELATED EMERGENCIES 67
 FIRE 67
 BLACKOUT 68
 DOMESTIC EMERGENCY 69
 BASIC SURVIVAL SKILLS 70
  Bonus Emergency Preparedness Kits *70*

CHAPTER 7: TRANSPORTATION & TRAVEL.. 73

 PUBLIC TRANSPORTATION 73
  Bus *73*
  Train/Trolley *74*
  Subway *74*
  Ferry *75*
  Uber/Lyft... *76*
  e-scooters *76*
  Time management.. *77*
 DRIVING 77
  Insurance & Registration *77*
  What to Keep in the Glove Box & Trunk *77*
  Regular Tune-Ups *78*
  If Your Car Breaks Down or Wrecks *78*
 FLYING & TRAVEL 78
  Booking Your Flight... *78*
  Packing Essentials... *79*
  Airport Security... *79*
  Boarding Tips.. *80*
  In-Flight Comfort... *80*
  Arrival & Baggage Claim... *81*
 SAFETY & COURTESY TIPS... 81
  Politeness on Transit... *81*
  Driving Courtesy.. *81*
  Staying Safe on Public Transport & Walking *82*
  Travel Safety *82*

CHAPTER 8: RELATIONSHIPS & COMMUNICATION 83

SOCIAL MEDIA 83
- *Privacy* 83
- *Online Communication* 84
- *Digital Balance* 84
- *Censorship* 84

ROOMMATES 84
- *Set Boundaries Early On* 84
- *Addressing Conflicts* 85
- *Privacy* 85

FRIENDS & FAMILY 85
- *Setting Expectations* 85
- *Difficult Conversations* 85
- *Mental Health* 86

COWORKERS & BOSSES 86
- *Professional Boundaries* 86
- *Say What You Need* 86
- *Handling Workplace Conflicts* 86

ROMANTIC RELATIONSHIPS 87
- *Early Boundaries* 87
- *Conflict* 87
- *Consent & Comfort* 87

NEIGHBORS 87
- *Being Friendly* 87
- *Issues* 88
- *Shared Spaces* 88

SETTING BOUNDARIES WITH YOURSELF 88
- *Knowing Your Limits* 88
- *Healthy Routines* 88
- *Self-Care* 89

CHAPTER 9: CAREER SKILLS 91

RESUME & PORTFOLIO 91
- *Crafting Your Resume* 91
- *Choosing the Right Resume Style* 91
- *Tailoring for Each Role* 92
- *Cover Letters* 92
- *Portfolio* 92

PROFESSIONAL ONLINE PROFILES 93
- *LinkedIn Basics* 93
- *Showcasing Your Skills* 93
- *Networking Do's & Don'ts* 93
- *Privacy & Professionalism* 93

JOB SEARCHING STRATEGIES 94
   Job Boards & Platforms 94
   Freelancing Platforms 94
   Scam Awareness 95
INTERVIEW TIPS 95
   Preparation Basics 95
   Dress Codes for In-Person & Remote Interviews 96
   Common Interview Questions & STAR Method 96
   Following Up 97
WORKPLACE DYNAMICS 98
   Knowing Generational Difference 98
   Workplace Etiquette 98
   Constructive Criticism 98
   Professional Boundaries 99
REMOTE & HYBRID WORK 99
   Productive Workspace 99
   Time Management & Accountability 99
   Communication Tools & Etiquette 99
   Work-Life Boundaries 100
GROWTH & DEVELOPMENT 100
   New Skills 100
   Mentors 100
   Career Goals 100
   Advocate for Yourself 100

CHAPTER 10: LISTS 101

NEW HOME NECESSITIES 101
CHORES 104
IMPORTANT DOCUMENTS 106
PREPAREDNESS 107
THE GO-TO FOR LISTS & TEMPLATES 108

CONCLUSION 109

ABOUT THE AUTHOR 111

REFERENCES 113

Introduction

Welcome to adulthood! After high school, I was excited but also really anxious. The freedom of being on my own sounded so awesome that I kind of forgot about all the responsibility that comes with it. If you're like I was back then, things like cleaning, laundry, cooking, bills, and finances sounded totally alien. Don't even get me started on making doctor appointments, renewing licenses, paying taxes, or dealing with landlords. It's overwhelming when you're used to parents handling it all, and now everything is up to you.

Okay, I'm sure you're wondering how to balance responsibilities and fun—will it just be endless work and chores?! No. It definitely doesn't have to be that mundane. With some planning and a few good habits thrown in, you'll be able to create free time for friends, hobbies, exploring, and making memories during this transition. Whether you're off to college, moving into your own place, starting a job, joining the military, or taking a gap year—this book will equip you with the skills to really feel like an independent adult. Building good routines now will seriously benefit you for years, potentially saving you tons of stress, money, and headaches later on.

We'll take on topics like cooking meals instead of eating out every day, doing laundry, cleaning tips, paying bills, basic home and car maintenance, filing taxes, personal finance and budgeting, self-care habits, staying organized, and lots more. If you're transitioning to college, trade schools, post-secondary programs, or the workforce, you'll find tips for crafting resumes and which loans work best for different types of education.

I promise adulting doesn't have to be as tedious as it sounds. I'll share plenty of productivity hacks so you're not wasting your precious free time on chores. There's even a way to schedule your week so you're not always scrambling. And I have no doubt that once you get the hang of balancing the "boring" stuff, you'll figure out adulting is actually pretty empowering. Yeah, even doing taxes.

It's also important to me that you don't see this guide as another rule book. It's meant to give you confidence for the many situations life throws at you. Trust me, nobody's perfect—we all struggle with routines and responsibility at times, no matter how old we are. So, my goal is to meet you where you're at, acknowledge that this transition is hard, and give you a supportive resource that motivates instead of overwhelms.

Let's start with some basic principles I wish I'd known:

- **Build healthy habits from the start:** There's a reason phrases like "old habits die hard" exist. When big changes happen, like leaving home for the first time, our brains are primed to absorb new patterns annoyingly fast. This is a huge opportunity to create routines that will make your life way smoother going forward. Do you want things like cleaning, self-care, healthy eating, exercise, and staying organized to feel normal? Or do you want to forever view them as endless chores? The choice is yours. Trying to retrain yourself down the line is so much harder than setting positive habits now. Consistency is all you need.

- **Be organized and plan ahead:** Chaos and last-minute scrambling might seem easier now—it might even be part of who you are—but feeling in control of your responsibilities will help out you and your mental health in the long run. Small things make a big difference. If you have weekly errands to run, try grouping them together with grocery shopping so everything gets done at once. Assign one or two cleaning tasks to certain days so your chores don't pile up. Use your favorite planning app or journal to plan your week, make to-do lists, and schedule time for things you love (like binging that new show). The easiest way to keep track of everything is by setting reminders on your phone. Think of structure as your safety net, not a straitjacket.

- **Balanced responsibilities and fun:** Figuring out a work-life balance has the potential to feel a tad impossible at this stage. Responsibilities will always be there, but happiness and fun are also musts—hobbies, social life, relaxing, and exploring new things! Block out regular times for both, like weeknights for studying and chores and weekends for fun. Use those scheduling tips to see the bigger picture, then reward yourself for getting tasks done. That way, you get treats for checking things off the adulting list, and you end up with more free time. It's a win-win.

- **Don't go it alone; lean on others:** No one can do everything on their own. Take it from me: asking for help is wise, not weak. Don't isolate yourself! Family, friends, community organizations, campus clubs, coworkers—whoever it may be, lean on them if life is too much. Odds are they'll relate to what you're going through. We all hit roadblocks, and you'll end up helping them in return someday. It's so important to stay connected, social, and open to advice. You never know who may end up in your life forever. Think of it as a future story to laugh about together.

- **Practice self-compassion:** Major changes unleash big emotions. Cut yourself some slack throughout the ups and downs. Little victories matter most. And yes, standards are necessary, but make sure they aren't so high that they cause you to spiral over mistakes—we're all learning. Laughing at yourself is healthier than harsh criticism. It's okay to tell your inner critic to shut up sometimes! Mental wellness looks different for everyone, so find what fills your cup. Make that a priority when you're feeling emotionally drained. Self-care isn't selfish—actually, it's a necessity.

I've started with these foundational principles because if you can absorb them early, you'll establish a great mindset. Think of it like a mental success compass that'll make your 20s and beyond a lot easier. The rest of the book will dig into topics like:

- Home and living skills.
- Basic repairs and maintenance.
- Health, wellness, and personal safety.
- Budget and finances.
- Emergency preparedness.
- Self-care and wellness.
- Communication and relationships.
- Career skills.
- And more.

These areas will offer the building blocks for you to take control, stay on track, and ultimately focus your time and energy on the fun parts of this stage of life—and there will be plenty! I really hope you're able to find value within these pages.

If nothing else, please remember: adulting is a constant work in progress, and there are many ways to do it. Be kind to yourself every step of the journey. I have complete faith in your ability to thrive as long as you stay true to who you are and don't lose heart.

Chapter 1:

Life Skills & Habits

I'm betting those daydreams of finally living somewhere without parents never included things like laundry and vacuuming. But if we want comfy places to eat, sleep, and chill, someone's got to look after the day-to-day stuff. The good news is that learning to manage your living space and schedule is totally within reach.

Kicking things off, your residence is going to be your main base as an adult. Whether it's a dorm, apartment, or maybe even your first home, routines will make it feel like an oasis.

I know most of us are far from neat freaks, so don't panic!

Time Management & Time Robbers

When schedules get packed, it's easy to lose track of time until you're super stressed and struggling to catch up. It might feel like you have all the time in the world now, but it disappears when commitments pile up. Before trying fancy planners, start by understanding how you really spend your day. Be honest about where your time vanishes. Is it scrolling endlessly, gaming, binge-watching, or procrastinating until panic mode kicks in? Seriously, no judgment. Identifying your biggest time-wasters is the first step toward change.

Don't sweat it if you catch yourself losing precious minutes. We've all been there! It's not about cutting out fun, just hitting pause before you zone out for hours on end. Balance is key, which means knowing when to block out distractions and focus. As you build awareness, you'll naturally create better habits—no harsh rules required.

Ready to tackle your time-wasters and improve your routine? Start by narrowing down some unproductive habits you might be falling into. Here are a few common ones to look out for:

- **Endless social media scrolling:** We all get sucked in, especially when tired. But mindlessly surfing distracts from deeper focus.

- **Marathon TV or streaming sessions:** Sure, it's cozy, but before you know it, the day is over with nothing of substance accomplished.

- **Zoning out vs intentional relaxation:** Zombie staring at a screen for hours isn't the same as blocking out time for naps, favorite shows, or doing something you enjoy.

- **Procrastinating chores:** This just leads to a stressful and potentially gross living area that takes a whole day to clean up.

- **Overthinking:** You're far from alone on this one, but be careful you don't overthink yourself into decision paralysis.

- **Socializing without intention:** Hanging out just to avoid FOMO usually gives *I want those hours back* vibes instead of *that was awesome* vibes.

Be real with yourself—do any patterns ring true? Don't feel bad about recognizing areas to grow. That's just a constant part of life in general. Spotting the time-sucking patterns now means you can take baby steps to correct them instead of trying to drop everything cold turkey.

Now that you've thought about any unproductive patterns in your routine, here are some things to keep in mind in establishing good routines:

- **Block your time:** Set aside an hour or two every day specifically for chores, exercise, and relaxing. This is how you can still enjoy things like gaming and binge-watching—give yourself small windows of time for fun things.

- **Prioritize top tasks:** List your top three tasks for the day and focus on those over worrying about the small stuff. You'll feel more accomplished even if you don't have time for extra chores.

- **Batch similar tasks:** Out of clean pants? Dedicate the day to laundry. Have to return something? Run all your errands for the week. Tackling email responses? Clean up your digital clutter, too.

- **Schedule buffers:** Structure is incredible, but life happens. Leave some buffer time in your routine so unexpected events don't throw you completely off track.

- **Celebrate small wins:** Treat yourself! If you've had a productive habit run, celebrate it. Have a movie night with your favorite snacks, or get your favorite coffee on the way to work. Even small wins deserve recognition.

Whether you decide to use all of these tips or none of them, just remember that routines shouldn't feel like a cage. Habits that help you knock out adulting priorities give you more flexibility to enjoy the spontaneous stuff—like knowing your favorite shirt is clean when you get invited to a last-minute concert.

Here are a few ways to start practicing time blocking:

Digital:

- Calendar reminders—use different colors to group types of activities.

- To-do list apps if you like to see tasks getting checked off in real time.

- Habit trackers if you need more accountability.

- General notes app if you want more freedom in how you structure your planning.

Analog:

- Planners with monthly and weekly templates.
- Sticky notes for daily reminders.
- Bullet journals that match your personality.
- Wall calendar for bigger picture visuals.

Keyboard, pencil, or a combination of both—all that matters is finding a system that works for you. If you don't like a method, you probably won't stick with it, so try out different things until you realize you're looking forward to checking that chore off the list or updating your planner with a new event. Small steps!

Household Chores, Utilities, & How-To's

I know chores and electric companies probably aren't top of mind when you think of fun independence, but they're a necessary evil. You'll feel a ton better if your environment isn't total chaos that runs on borrowed Wi-Fi from your neighbor. Let's start with the biggest hurdles—laundry, dishes, meal planning, and utilities. It's not as daunting as it sounds, especially once you learn how "mini chores" will save you hours of time every week.

Laundry

You shouldn't have to learn laundry room procedures through trial and error, aka "the hard way." Not all washing machines are created equal and not all detergents will get out stains. To save your clothes, towels, and bedding from potential disaster, here are some laundry guidelines:

- Right from the jump, you have to get familiar with your washer/dryer. If it's older, do a few test runs with towels or old sheets to make sure there's no funny business. If it's newer, take the time to figure out the settings. Sometimes, the automatic wash cycle isn't your friend.

- If you have room, get multiple laundry baskets to keep your clothes sorted. One basket for clothes that can go in the dryer, one for line-dry, and one for white clothes is a good place to start, but there are several methods of sorting to choose from. Find a sorting and basket system that fits your wardrobe.

- Check the labels to see if anything needs to be line-dried, washed inside out, or flat-out should never see the inside of a washing machine. Separate those items into their appropriate basket or sort everything in the moment.

- Most loads of laundry will recommend cold water but always check the water temperature so you don't wash all your favorites in hot water and potentially shrink everything.

- Just like with clothes, give your towels and bedding their own wash cycle.

- No matter what you're washing, don't overstuff the washer or dryer. A washer that's too full could break, overflow, or leave you with detergent-splotched clothes. A dryer that's too full will take forever at best, and it could even burn your clothes or catch on fire at worst.

- Invest in a detergent, fabric softener, and dryer sheet brand you like. Just because something is on super sale isn't a great reason to buy it... if it doesn't get your clothes clean, it was not worth those few dollars you saved. The better you take care of your stuff, the longer it will last.

- If you forgot to take things out of the washer for a few days, do a serious smell check. If there's any hint of mildew, run it again.

- Ideally, laundry will get folded and hung up right when it comes out of the dryer to avoid wrinkles. In the real world, get yourself a good iron or a small steamer to fix wrinkles on the fly.

- Bleach is not the be-all-end-all solution for stains! Even on white clothes, be careful. Look for stain removers that help remove very specific things—ketchup, makeup, grass, dairy, oil. It never hurts to have extra stain removers around.

- Dry cleaning. This can be tricky because sometimes you can get away with washing certain items in a laundry bag on a delicate cycle. When in doubt, listen to the tag and find a reliable dry cleaner in your area.

If laundry feels like your mortal enemy, try blocking out a whole day every two weeks and do all of it in one go. Maybe you break up clothes and bedding on alternate weeks. To "trick" your brain into not disliking it so much, reward yourself with episodes of a show while you're waiting on cycles to finish up or plan on getting your favorite takeout instead of cooking that day. At the very least, how great is it to put on warm clothes straight from the dryer?

Dishes

Moving on to the kitchen for some dishwashing wisdom. Whether you lucked out with a new dishwasher or yours has a mind of its own, here are some basic pointers:

- Scrape and rinse your plates before loading them into the dishwasher. It's a dishwasher, not a garbage disposal.

- Small items like cups and smaller dishes on top. Bigger things like plates and baking dishes on the bottom. The lesser-known tip is to make sure glassware is snug so it doesn't fall over and break during the cycle. Broken glass in a dishwasher is not fun to clean up.

- Even worse than broken dishware is melted or otherwise ruined items. Not everything is dishwasher safe—like certain nonstick cookware—so double-check before you toss it in.

- Don't overload the dishwasher. If water can't get to it, it can't be cleaned. It's a common misconception that dishwashers fill all the way up with water (they don't). Make sure the spray arms can do their job.

- Detergent matters, especially how much and where it goes. There's usually one spot for a detergent dispenser and one for a rinse aid. It definitely matters to know which is which. If this part is worrisome, detergent pods can save you a lot of worry, but they cost more, so you'll have to decide if they are worth it for your circumstances.

- Rinse aids aren't necessary, but they are nice for keeping water spots to a minimum. Something to think about if you favor a lot of glassware.

- It's very gross, but check your food trap once a month or so. If you start noticing puddles of water in the bottom of your dishwasher, the food trap is likely the culprit. Check the manual for instructions on how to clean the food trap and if there is a filter to be cleaned. Don't have the manual? Just google the make and model number, and you should be able to find the manual online.

- If you have a drying cycle, take advantage of it. Don't expect perfection here, but it helps.

- Speaking of drying, if you have to hand wash everything, a drying rack or mat will be your best friend. Keep a rotation of clean dish towels by your sink and arm yourself with a soap-dispensing scrubby.

The real secret to keeping up with dishes is annoying but effective—do them as you go. But we'll get more into that in the next section.

Mini Chores/Minimum Maintenance

There's a book I read years ago that changed my life called *Totally Organized the Bonnie McCullough Way* (a big inspiration for this book). That's where I learned "Minimum Maintenance" and never looked back. Basically, you take five to ten minutes per room just to declutter.

It's a small step before daily chores that makes things a lot easier and helps you out when things get stressful. Work to establish the habit of minimum maintenance before you go to bed every night. You will be surprised at how easy it is to keep your place looking great.

Think about times when life really throws you off schedule—finals, covering extra shifts, family emergencies, holidays. The list is pretty long. Daily minimum maintenance keeps your living space functional during those times when daily chores have to take a backseat. Coming home to a relatively clean area after a long day does a lot more for your mental well-being than you'd think.

Here are a few examples of daily mini chores with some estimated time frames:

- Declutter and wipe down surfaces, countertops, coffee tables, desks, bathroom vanity. (1-2 minutes per surface)

- Make your bed every morning, even if it's not perfect. (2-3 minutes)

- Put clean dishes away and wash any dirty dishes or load them in the dishwasher. (5 minutes)

- Put misplaced floor items back where they go—shoes back in the closet, throw pillows back on the couch, boxes from online orders in the recycle bin. (2-5 minutes)

- Do a quick check of the fridge and pantry for anything that might be expired. (2-3 minutes)

Doing yourself the favor of minimum maintenance means you won't end up stress-cleaning an hour before people come over. Don't forget, it's not about perfection. It's about creating a home where you feel safe, happy, and comfortable. Trust me; it's easier to feel that way when you don't have to worry about dirty dishes attracting gnats or aggravating your allergies from built-up dust. A few weekly chores to stay on top of will help:

- Grab a washable or disposable duster and go over the shelves, fan blades, door frames, and the top of your refrigerator. Pretty much any surface you don't really think about on a daily basis.

- Depending on how many flooring types you have, vacuum, sweep, and/or mop.

- Give the bathroom fixtures some extra attention. That means the toilet and shower—bathroom cleaners tend to have some intense fumes, so be mindful of that.

- Clean out your fridge, freezer, and pantry. Since your daily maintenance takes care of expired things, you'll just need to wipe down the shelves.

- Everyone needs their own version of a junk drawer. So, whatever you've chosen as your junk area, give that a good declutter.

Meal Planning

Now that you've got some tips for keeping your kitchen consistently clean (clean enough, anyway), it makes cooking much less stressful. Even if your cooking skills are limited to Ramen, meal planning will make your life easier. This is what saves you from buying a week's worth of random snacks that aren't actually meals. Doritos and sparkling water are delicious but aren't substantial enough to live off of.

Before we get to the tips, I want to point out the biggest cost factor that makes cooking feel more expensive than it is. Basic ingredients and spices—the cost adds up! If your budget allows you to stock up all at once, do it. If not, buy one or two things per shopping trip based on what you're cooking. Start with the essentials like flour, sugar, salt, and pepper.

Now for the meal planning tips:

- If you're short on time or not the best chef, pick simple recipes with a few ingredients. Think tacos or pasta—easy to make but still filling.

- Cooking for one is tough, so just make a little extra so you have leftovers for another night of the week. You can even freeze the leftovers for an easy meal next week.

- Make it fun with theme nights. Taco Tuesday is a classic, but you could spice it up with Macaroni Mondays or Stir-Fridays.

- Build a budget-friendly grocery list by planning your week with meals using similar ingredients. Sign up for your grocery store's rewards card or savings plan, too. Coupons are magical.

- If you need quick lunches or snacks throughout the week, see if you can prep anything during the weekend. Have your veggies pre-cut, make a big batch of rice for the week, assemble bags of fruit for easy smoothies—whatever saves future time.

- Before you make a shopping list, check what's already in your fridge and pantry. Look up fun recipes for any random ingredients for inspiration.

- Pick a night or two for takeout!

Understanding Utilities

A dreaded task of being a fully self-sufficient adult is dealing with utilities. Getting them set up is particularly irritating. Electricity, water, and gas are the main priorities, followed very closely by internet and your preferred way to watch TV. We'll start with the logistics of getting your new place connected. Almost every service will have a website where you can manage your account, but you may have to talk to a live human in the early stages.

Here's a good starting checklist:

- About two weeks before you move in is when you'll want to get the ball rolling. Your landlord, apartment management, or realtor will most likely have a list of service providers for you. If not, look up the electric, water, sewage, and gas companies for your area. Keep in mind that gas and sewage setups aren't necessary for every city.

- Check each provider's website to see what information they'll need before starting your service. It's obvious they'll need your name, address, and phone number, but sometimes they also ask for different forms of ID. In some cases, you may need to pay a deposit on the spot.

- Ask if they offer any discounted rates for first-time account setups, student discounts, or automatic payment savings.

- Internet providers are always promoting package deals for cable, streaming services, and even bundling phone plans. It doesn't hurt to see if anything applies to you, especially if you aren't on your family's phone plan anymore.

- These days, it's rare that someone will come to your home during the setup phase, even for internet. Always ask; that way, if someone shows up saying "they're with the company," you know whether or not to let them in. Better safe than sorry!

- Use strong passwords for each account and save them somewhere secure, like one of the many password-saving apps. There's nothing worse than forgetting your Wi-Fi password.

Once you're up and running, here are some bill-paying best practices:

- Paperless is easier for everyone involved and also better for the planet. All of your service provider billing will be managed online, anyway.

- Autopay takes some due-date stress off your plate. Just make sure to set reminders so your bank account can always handle the payment.

- Sign up for usage alerts. Any excessive use of water, electricity, gas, internet, or data could spike your monthly bill. The alerts help you budget for that.

- Doing yearly research to see if there are replacement providers that can give you better rates is a decent way to rack up savings. Make sure you read the fine print before making a switch, though.

- If you aren't home a lot during certain hours, adjust your thermostat to a lower setting while you're gone. If the weather is nice, you can even leave it off.

- LED bulbs use 90% less energy for the same light output over time. Lightbulbs aren't cheap, so choose wisely.

- Older windows leak, which can have a very unfortunate effect on your AC and heating bills. If you notice any draftiness, grab some caulk or give your maintenance crew a call.

Chapter 2:

Home Repair, Decor, & Safety

There's a lot you can do to take care of your living space, but sometimes stuff just breaks. And it usually happens at the most inconvenient time possible. Surprises like that really mess up your plans and your budget.

Now, it's safe to say you've used a plunger before or at least know the basic mechanics. There are less common problems than a clogged toilet, though. Pipes causing problems, finicky air filters, and shelves falling off the wall. Not to mention what to do if your dinner suddenly bursts into flames.

Keeping your home maintenance in check is kind of like brushing your teeth. It's not life or death if you miss a day, but skip a month, and you're looking at a mouth full of dental disasters. Good habits, helpful hacks, and safety know-how go a long way.

Plumbing

If you're renting, plumbing is usually a "call the landlord" situation, but there are still minor issues you can handle yourself. If you own your place, you're fully responsible, but that doesn't mean you have to be a pro plumber. The key is knowing which jobs you can handle with a plunger or a little baking soda and which ones are better left to the pros.

Toilets

We've all been there—a toilet that just won't flush. Usually, a plunger will do the trick, but there are a couple of bonus options just in case.

- **Plunger:** This is your go-to first step. Make sure to use a toilet plunger (the one with a flange) and plunge your heart out for 10-15 seconds. Nine times out of ten, this will work.

- **Baking soda and vinegar:** If the plunger isn't cutting it, pour about a cup of baking soda followed by a cup of vinegar down the toilet. Let it fizz for a few minutes, then quickly pour in hot (not boiling) water. The bubbles can break down clogs.

- **Dish soap and hot water:** No baking soda or vinegar? Pour about 1/4 cup of dish soap into the toilet, let it sit for a bit, and then follow with hot (again, not boiling) water. The soap lubricates the pipes, helping the clog slide out.

Faucets

Faucets can be tricky, especially if you're a renter. This is one of those projects that can go horribly wrong very quickly, so make sure you're up to the task and have all the right tools. If you're feeling brave, watch a how-to video, grab the right tools, and take lots of pictures of the faucet and plumbing setup before diving in. Someone at your local hardware store can help you find replacement gaskets, o-rings, and washers before you take everything apart.

- **Tools needed:** You'll want a wrench (probably a basin wrench), screwdriver, pliers, and possibly some replacement parts like washers or o-rings.

- **Basic steps:** First, turn off the water supply (very important!). Next, disassemble the faucet to check for worn-out parts, like washers or o-rings, and replace them. Reassemble carefully.

- **Potential disaster plan:** If water sprays everywhere, or it seems like you're making it worse, stop. Try tightening everything back up and calling a plumber (or your landlord) before it gets messier. A small leak can turn into a flood fast.

Drains

If you find yourself standing in too many inches of water while you're showering, then your drain probably needs help.

- **Drain cleaner:** Always follow the instructions carefully, and don't mix different types of cleaners—you could end up with a toxic fumes scenario.

- **Drain snake:** For tougher clogs, try a drain snake. It's a very cheap plastic option with little teeth to snag all the gross stuff in your drain. Insert it down the drain, twist it to catch the blockage, and pull it out. Be prepared for splatter, though...

- **Baking soda and vinegar:** If it worked on the toilet, give it a whirl on the drain. Pour about a half cup of each down the drain, let it bubble, and rinse with hot water after a few minutes.

Frozen Pipes & ACs

Frozen pipes are no joke, and they can royally mess up your living space. Prevention is always ideal, but dealing with frozen plumbing is something most people deal with.

- **Prevention:** Keep the thermostat above 50°F, open the cabinet doors under sinks, and let faucets drip on extremely cold nights to keep the water moving. Wrap your pipes in sleeves if you want to go the extra mile.

- **Already frozen:** Turn off the water supply and apply mild heat to slowly thaw them out—a hairdryer is your go-to here. Check for any leaks or cracks as you go and call a plumber or landlord if it's looking dicey.

Leaky Wall/Floor/Ceiling

If you notice water dripping from a wall, floor, or ceiling, call a plumber or call your landlord. Full stop. Home Depot can't help you here. This kind of leak is usually tied to bigger issues within the plumbing system or building structure, and it's best handled by a professional.

Electrical

You probably won't have to worry about much more than deciding which brand of light bulbs you like best, but it's good to be aware of other electrical basics. This is a good area to know your limits—it's okay if your limit is lightbulbs.

Light Fixtures

Here's where bulb know-how comes in handy. If you're feeling daring, you can also switch out light fixtures—just not if you're a renter.

- **Bulbs:** Easy fix. Turn off the switch first and check the wattage recommendation so you don't overload it. For any weirdly shaped bulbs like the ones in track lights, take the old one to the store with you so you buy the right kind.

- **Exposed wires:** If you spot exposed wires or any fraying, don't mess with them. Put the electrical tape down. It's not worth getting shocked. Call an electrician if you own or maintenance if you rent.

- **Replacing fixtures:** The ease of replacement depends on how old your light fixture is. Be ready for some odd surprises if you live in a dated house (been there). Your new light fixture should come with directions, but finding how-to videos always helps. Grab a friend to help, and don't forget to cut the power to the fixture you're working on.

Useless Light Switches

You've probably encountered one at some point—those switches that don't seem to do anything. Sometimes, they have secret functions. Sometimes, they're just a mystery with no resolution.

- **Testing outlets:** Try plugging your phone charger (with your phone attached) into different outlets, then flip the mystery switch on to see if your phone starts charging. It's a tedious process, but it might pay off. Check random garage and outdoor outlets, too.

- **Still a mystery:** If you've checked everything and it still seems useless, it probably is. No need to mess with it further unless it's buzzing or feels warm (in that case, call a professional).

Circuit breaker

The circuit breaker is the heart of your electrical setup. If you don't know where it is, go locate it. In houses, they're almost always in basements or garages. In apartments, try looking for a metal door set into the wall in one of the most inconvenient spots imaginable.

- **Circuit panel:** Your circuit panel has switches (or breakers) that control power in different areas. They should be labeled with each room the switch controls, but that's not a guarantee. Get familiar with them, and label them if you can.

- **Tripped breakers:** If you lose power in part of your house, it's usually because a breaker tripped. To fix it, find the switch that's out of alignment with the rest and flip it all the way off, then back on. Or find the switch to the room without power then flip it off and then back on. If you've lost power to the whole house, that's likely not a breaker issue. More on that later.

- **Power limit:** Overloading your circuits by plugging in too many high-wattage things at once can trip your breakers or even cause more intense electrical issues. Try to pay attention to which outlets and appliances are on each breaker and spread things out to avoid overload.

Warning signs

Okay, not every electrical issue is a five-alarm fire, but certain signs could mean it's time to call an electrician. It's better to be on the safe side than ignore them.

- **Flickering lights:** If lights flicker occasionally, it's usually harmless. For consistent *Stranger Things* flickering, check the bulb first. If it's fine, you'll need to call a professional to fix the issue.

- **Sparks:** It's not a good sign to see sparks when you plug something in, especially if it happens more than once. Unplug it, and don't use that outlet until it's been checked.

- **Buzzing outlets:** Outlets shouldn't make noise or feel warm. Buzzing, warmth, or discoloration—stop using that outlet and get it looked at ASAP.

Home Improvement

Turning your space into something that feels like *yours* doesn't require a complete makeover. A few small changes make a big impact, even if you're just fixing a squeaky door or hanging a few pictures.

Basic Tools

Your life plan may include never touching a hammer. That's fine. But if you want any of your DIY-inclined friends to help, have the tools they need ready.

- **Hammer:** Go with a good brand, it's worth it.

- **Screwdriver set:** It should have both flathead and Phillips screwdrivers in a couple of sizes.

- **Adjustable wrench:** Or a wrench set—great for bolts, pipes, and tightening or loosening odd-sized nuts.

- **Tape measure:** You'll need to measure stuff. That pretty much covers it.

- **Level:** This is a no-brainer for hanging shelves and frames.

- **Utility knife:** Handy for opening packages, trimming wallpaper, or scoring peel-and-stick flooring.

Cabinets & Doors

Ever open a cabinet, and the door fully comes off? Expect a few squeaky hinges, wobbly doorknobs, and cabinet doors to make your morning more interesting.

- **Squeaks and rust:** A little WD-40, coconut oil, or even bar soap can help with squeaky hinges. Rust can be a little trickier, and the hinges may need a full-on replacement. Fortunately, most hinges are easy to replace by taking them to the hardware store and finding a match.

- **Screws and hinges:** Reiterating how important it is to take the hinge with you to the store, especially if you're replacing a bunch at once. If you just want to clean them, you can also try soaking them in warm, soapy water or vinegar for about 30 minutes. Be careful not to get stabbed by any screws in the process.

- **Fixing or Replacing Doorknobs:** Wobbly doorknobs can typically be fixed with a quick tightening of the screws. If it's too far gone, a new upgrade is fairly inexpensive and easy to install.

Pictures

It's not really your home without your favorite wall art, but that doesn't mean your walls have to be riddled with holes, either. There are ways around losing your deposit because you hung a few photos.

- **Nail and hammer hack:** Put a piece of masking tape on the back of your picture frame. Use a pen to mark a dot where the nail should go (especially helpful if your frame has two spots for nails). Transfer the tape to the wall, and now you know exactly where to hammer the nail. Remove the tape. Done.

- **Renting solution:** Command hooks. There are about a million options, so you should be able to find something that works for you. If you're hanging something lightweight that shows the hanging source, try some decorative thumbtacks that only leave small holes.

- **Heavy stuff:** Best to avoid command hooks for super heavy frames or mirrors. A hole in the wall is better than a hole in *you* if it falls. Look for specialty hooks that can hold 50-100+ lbs.

Curtains

Obviously, curtains are great for privacy and adding a little extra pizazz. Another fun fact is that heavier curtains can also help prevent draftiness from older windows. Shoot for blackout curtains if you're sunlight-averse in the morning.

- **Tools needed:** Curtain rods, wall anchors, a level, a drill, and screws. A lot of curtain rods will come with everything you need, but sometimes the wall anchors provided are flimsy and less than ideal. You can absolutely hang curtains just using a screwdriver, but a drill will make things much easier. Make sure the rod is the right size for the window and the curtains are the right length.

- **Space illusions:** If you aren't lucky enough to live in a space with 10-foot ceilings, you can make your space look taller with curtains. Mount your curtain rods very close to the ceiling or even on the ceiling for the illusion of visual height. Don't forget to measure how long the curtain panels need to be. It won't have the same effect if your curtains are hanging two feet off the ground. Buy rods that are wider than needed so that your curtain panels hang on either side of the window when they are open without covering any of the glass... Presto! Your windows now look much larger than they actually are!

Shelves

Shelves are perfect for storage and decor, but there's no renter-friendly way to hang floating shelves. Sorry renters, you'll have to weigh the pros and cons of holey walls here.

- **Tools and wall studs:** You'll want a stud finder, a drill, and a level. Hopefully, your shelves come with anchors and screws—if not, off to the hardware store. Regardless of how much weight your shelves will hold, utilize the studs or get specialty wall anchors. Drywall alone isn't reliable.

- **Standing shelves:** This is an underused trick, but secure your standing shelves to the wall with brackets or safety straps. Earthquakes, kids, cats... all things that can easily tip over a shelving unit.

Heating/Cooling

There are a few things you can do to help out your heating and cooling systems, especially when the weather hits extremes. But it's always best to get a professional or call your landlord for major HVAC issues. Even if you're studying to become a heating and cooling specialist, fixing things yourself could end up backfiring.

- **Changing filters:** Dirty filters make your system work harder, meaning you won't get as much AC, and you're also breathing in dusty air. If you live in an apartment complex, they'll usually provide the filters if you ask. Change your filter every few months, depending on usage, pets, or allergies. Most systems have an easily accessible filter slot near the intake vent. Pull out the old filter, slide in a new one, and you're done.

- **Window unit care:** If you have a window AC unit, turn it off (don't remove it from the window) and use a duster or soft cloth to clean the vents and controls. A vacuum with a brush attachment works great for this, too. Most window units have a removable filter you can rinse with soap and water. Let it dry completely before putting it back in—mold growth is real.

- **Frozen AC filter:** This is a summer issue that usually affects apartments more than houses. If you aren't getting any circulating cool air, remove the intake cover and check out the filter. If the pipes or filter are solid white, that is ice. Break out the hairdryer and ask maintenance to bring you a new filter.

- **Warning signs:** Strange noises, unpleasant smells, inconsistent temperatures, or units that keep turning on and off repeatedly are all red flags. Even if things seem fine, scheduling an annual inspection with a professional can catch small problems before they become expensive issues. Renters should automatically get this service yearly, so keep that in mind.

Appliances

This is less about taking a screwdriver to your appliance and more about making sure the ick factor stays to a minimum. A good deep clean does more to keep your appliances working smoothly than you'd think.

Fridge

Besides making sure there aren't any dishes growing civilizations of mold in the fridge, there are some other basic upkeep items.

- **Ice maker and water filter:** Every few months, change out the water filter if your fridge has a water dispenser. For ice makers, it's a good idea to give those a deep clean every six months or so. There's no need to disassemble the actual ice-making mechanics; just dump out the ice cubes and give the easy-to-reach places some attention.

- **Shelves and drawers:** Spills happen, so wipe shelves and drawers out every few weeks before they turn into concerningly sticky problems.

Dishwasher

Just because it cleans dishes doesn't mean it's self-cleaning.

- **Clean the filter:** You might remember this from Chapter 1, but food bits can clog the filter, so give it a rinse every month. Just twist it out from the bottom and rinse it under warm water.

- **Vinegar cycle:** Pour a cup of vinegar into the bottom of the dishwasher and run it on an empty hot cycle to get rid of grime and weird smells.

- **Gunky spray arms:** If your dishes aren't getting very clean, check for food particles stuck in the spray holes. Use a toothpick to clean them out.

Oven

Unless you've severely burnt your dinner, ovens shouldn't smoke every time you use them. Put a large baking sheet under dishes that could overflow to save the bottom of your oven from baked-on disasters.

- **Self-cleaning cycle:** If your oven has this function (most do), run it every few months to burn off sludge. Make sure you open a window or run a fan because it can get smoky. If it gets too smoky, though, turn the cycle off.

- **Manual Cleaning:** For ovens without self-cleaning or if that feature is way too smoky, you can make a paste with baking soda and water. Slather it on the inside, let it sit for a few hours, and wipe it clean. There are also oven cleaners you can buy at the store.

Microwave

The microwave sees a lot of action, which means it also sees a lot of food splatter. Caked-on food that eventually clogs the vents can mean the death of your microwave and can potentially be a fire hazard.

- **Steam clean:** This is by far the easiest option, which is why it's the only one here. Fill a microwave-safe bowl with water and a few lemon slices, heat it up for a few minutes, and let the steam loosen any stuck-on food. Wipe *everything* down really well afterward, and you should be all set. You can throw the turntable in the dishwasher for good measure.

Toaster/Toaster Oven

If it smells like your kitchen is on fire every time you make toast, that's a solid indicator to give the toaster a good clean. Aluminum foil is your best friend for toaster ovens.

- **Crumb tray and racks:** Most toaster ovens have a removable tray at the bottom. Slide it out, dump the crumbs, and give it a scrub. Steel wool is great for getting the racks clean.

- **Shake it out:** It's clearly not wise to wash your toaster with soap and water. Give it a gentle shake over the sink to knock out any lingering crumbs. If you notice something stuck to the heating coils, it may be time for a new toaster.

Vacuum

Emptying the dustbin when it's full isn't the only secret to a long vacuum life. Every now and then, it deserves a spa day.

- **Clean the filter:** Many vacuums have a washable filter. Check your manual, but you should be able to rinse it out in the sink every few months.

- **Tubes and brush roll:** If your vacuum easily comes apart for cleaning purposes, give any tubes a good rinse in case they're clogged. It also helps to cut away anything entwined in the brush roll. It's gross but necessary. Just make sure everything is completely dry before reassembling.

Safety

Fires and break-ins are very unfortunate possibilities, but you can give yourself some extra layers of warnings and safety. We cover a lot more emergency preparedness in Chapter 6, so this is just for daily safety.

Smoke Detectors

Smoke detectors *should* already be installed wherever you live. Whether they're installed or not, consider getting/replacing detectors with heat sensors instead of smoke sensors. If you're prone to creating smoke signals in the kitchen, you might get tired of fanning the detector with a pillow until it quiets down. Heat-sensitive detectors do exactly what they sound like. They detect heat and alert you if it's a dangerous situation.

- **When to check:** Test smoke detectors monthly by pressing the "test" button. If they're working correctly, they'll make an obnoxiously loud beep that will terrify any nearby pets.

- **When to replace:** Change the batteries twice a year, ideally when you change your clocks for daylight saving time. If you stick around the same house for a while, replace the whole unit every 10 years to keep things up to date.

Fire Extinguishers & Blankets

A good rule of thumb is to keep an extinguisher and backup fire blanket in the kitchen, but if you have a multi-story house, keep one on each floor. Fire blankets should be more common. Just in case it's not obvious, a fire blanket isn't the same as the knit throw on your sofa.

- **Fire extinguishers:** Know how to use them—remember "PASS:" Pull the pin, Aim at the base, Squeeze the handle, Sweep from side to side. Check the gauge monthly to make sure it's fully charged, and snag a new one if it's empty.

- **Fire blankets:** These are a great backup for small grease or stove fires. They're super easy to use—just pull it out, put it over the flames, and it smothers the fire.

- **Bonus tips:** Use a pot lid to smother small stovetop fires. Baking soda can also smother small fires in a pinch. Never use water on grease or electrical fires!

Security Systems

If it's in the budget, invest in a security system. You may have to check with your complex or landlord if you're renting, but apartments can have security systems, too. There are even more budget-friendly options.

- **Alarm systems:** Find a company you like and trust. The next step is setting up your security panel and attaching little sensors to your doors and windows. Most systems let you control everything through an app and automatically notify the authorities when the alarm is triggered.

- **Cameras:** If a whole system isn't feasible, a little camera can deter quite a bit. Anything by your front or back door to give anyone pause before trying anything sketchy. Honestly, even a fake camera can help—intruders don't have to know it's not hooked up.

- **Security bars:** These are an especially great option for renters or anyone not living in the safest of neighborhoods. They make security bars for doors that rest underneath the doorknob for extra resistance against forced entry. If you have a large sliding glass patio door, they also have security bars to lay in the track between the door and the wall so it can't be opened from the outside. You can use a broomstick in a pinch.

If the extinguisher or fire blanket isn't enough. If you hear anyone trying to enter your house or hear suspicious noises outside. If you hear violence or gunshots. Call 911. Know your exits if it's a fire. Stay put somewhere safe until the authorities get there for other situations.

Chapter 3:

Health, Wellness, & First Aid

You can have the swankiest living space in the world, but what good is that if your health takes a dive? I get it—health and wellness can be a stressful topic because it covers *a lot*. So, let's break it down a little bit.

Daily hygiene habits go without saying, but we're going to say them anyway. Then you've got your nutrition, fitness, and basic first aid. All of these things directly impact your mental health, making it one of the most important things to keep an eye on.

It's hard to enjoy being independent if you're feeling anxious, depressed, or generally unwell. That's why we also cover the benefits of health insurance, even though it is now and always will be endlessly confusing. Sorry, no helpful hacks for that one.

I promise these healthy habits will pay off big in the long run. Your well-being should always come first, so don't feel bad about prioritizing it.

Hygiene

This doesn't need to be lengthy, but it does deserve a quick mention. It's not just about "feeling clean." Good hygiene affects your health, confidence, and how other people interact with you.

The Basics

- **Showers/Baths:** Showering every day is a no-brainer. It's not like the hygiene police will arrest you for missing a day now and then, but it's a good habit for a lot of reasons. Hair care will vary for everyone—if it looks or feels generally icky, it's probably best to throw shampoo on that situation. Dry shampoo can also be a lifesaver if you lean more toward the oily side. If showering isn't your favorite activity, try out different soaps, scrubs, or loofas to make it feel more like a spa experience than something to just 'get through.'

- o **Pro tip:** Go ahead and Q-Tip your ears right when you get out of the shower. The steam helps loosen up the crud, making it easier to clean. But DO NOT insert them into your ear canal.

- **Dental hygiene:** Have you ever been talking to someone and wished you had a mint to offer them? It's flat-out impossible to stay minty fresh 24 hours a day, but twice a day brushing helps prevent awkward scenarios like that. Since flossing is time-consuming and annoying, try using a water pick to speed things up. If you haven't found a mouthwash you like yet, buy them in travel sizes first until you find your favorite.

- **Skincare:** Most of us have had the joy of dealing with finicky skin. Even if you're lucky enough to enjoy a clear complexion, a skincare routine will help keep it that way. There's no need to go all out with a 10-step skincare plan, but your older self will thank you for taking care of your face. Sunscreen is your best friend every day, no matter if it's sunny or not. Trust me. And keeping any unruly eyebrow hair in check can also help you look more polished.

- **Nails:** No matter what length you prefer fingernails (real or not), keep them clean. If there's always muck in your nail beds and under your nails, it implies that you don't wash your hands, which isn't a good look. You get more of a pass if you're industry requires you to work with paint, oil, or other clingy substances that are hard to scrub off. Toenails—whether there's someone in your bed or not, it's generally better to avoid having talons, so trim them regularly.

- **Deodorant:** Find your favorite and slather it on every single day. Aluminum-free deodorants are ideal, but they aren't always the best at preventing sweat. There's nothing wrong with going the opposite direction and choosing a clinical strength option. Figure out your armpit preferences and load up the right products for you. All-over body deodorants are popular, too.

- **On-the-go hygiene kit:** A small travel kit will help you out in tons of situations. How many times have you been driving down the road and realized you forgot to put deodorant on? Life. Hit up the travel section and stock up a small bag that can live in your bag or your car.

  - Deodorant
  - Floss
  - Mouthwash
  - Mints/gum
  - Dry shampoo
  - Nail clipper
  - Q-Tips
  - Tweezers

One final note on hygiene. I think we've all seen people who don't wash their hands after they use the bathroom, and it should go without saying—gross.

Nutrition

Fast food is way easier after a long day, and that's totally fine on occasion. Making that a daily habit can come back to bite you in multiple ways, though. Learning to balance drive-thrus and eating at home is a skill. It'll definitely help your wallet, and your arteries will thank you later, too.

Fast Food

Let's start with the money side of things. Eating out adds up crazy fast. I know Frostys are legendary—you deserve one every now and then. But did you know the average fast-food meal is between $10–15? Multiply that by three meals a day, seven days a week, 30 days a month. Even at the lowest cost of $10, you're looking at $6,300 a month on food!

Yes, it's extreme to think you would eat out to that extent, but it's still food for thought. Pun intended. You should set aside some funds for going to your favorite brunch spot with friends or grabbing a quick burger on your way home from work from time to time but put a limit on how many days you treat yourself.

Cooking at Home

It may seem that if you have to buy every single ingredient for one meal, the cost doesn't feel worth the result. That's part of the deal when you're building up your kitchen ingredient supply—no way around it.

There are still ways to save. Are you a protein smoothie person? A container of protein, a bunch of frozen bananas, and a jar of peanut butter will set you up for at least a week or two of breakfasts. Think of how much one smoothie from your favorite smoothie bar costs compared to the one in your kitchen. More of a breakfast sandwich person? Loaf of bread, a dozen eggs, and a pack of cheese slices. That's at least eight sandwiches for the cost of one or two at a restaurant. Cereal? So many options. So many breakfasts. So little money spent.

Plus, some of that money you save can be put aside for the eating-out fund.

Nutritional Evaluation of Each

It's tough to know what's actually "organic" or "good for you" these days. If you get too focused on only eating things that are 100% good for you all the time... you'll be hungry. It's more important to focus on doing the best you can with what you have.

Sometimes life puts you in a spot where you're reliant on fast food or takeout for long periods of time. Unfortunately, most drive-thru takeout is loaded with sodium, saturated fat, and added sugars—not great for your long-term health. Try to vary what you order so it doesn't include fried breading, excess sugar, or blatantly artificial ingredients every day. Trading out a soda for water will do wonders. Also, salads do exist in fast food but trust your judgment about where to avoid them.

Cooking at home gives you more control over what goes into your meals. You can choose recipes that include fresh veggies or leaner proteins. When snagging pre-made ingredients, be sure to check those labels... trust me. It's still insanely easy to eat junk seven days a week at home but think you're eating well. Just because you made it at home doesn't mean it's healthy. Maybe cooking isn't and never will be your thing. That's okay. There are premade meal options that are still better than eating fast food every night.

Find the balance that works for you and keep an eye on what you're fueling up with. If you feel sluggish all the time, take a look at your diet and see if anything can be adjusted for the better.

Cooking Tips

- **Start with what you like:** Look up recipes for what you're craving. If you're missing Taco Bell, make a crunch wrap supreme at home—it's easier than you'd think. If you want more of a challenge, try a salmon filet with sauteed veggies. Look for recipes with step-by-step videos!

- **Master one or two things:** Once you've found a few recipes you like, keep practicing them until you're comfortable making them on your own. Scrambled eggs and buttered noodles totally count, by the way.

- **Ask for help:** Recruit taste-testers, see if friends or family can donate cookware, bribe someone to stir your soup while you take a break. Whatever it is, asking for help is better than the possibility of a ruined meal.

- **Use what you have:** This doesn't apply if your pantry consists of a lonely jar of peas that was there when you moved in. If you're decently stocked, look for apps that let you type in what you have and give you recipes based on that list. It's a fun way to try something new and will stretch your grocery budget for the week.

- **Bonus tips:** If it smells weird, don't eat it. If any portion of bread has mold on it, throw it away. Can-openers cannot be replaced by knives—don't do it.

Fitness

You have learned to cook potatoes, but there's no reason to turn into one. Any kind of general exercise will help you feel better and keep stress levels down. The biggest problem tends to be finding time for it, especially when you're juggling a busy schedule. Good news—you can literally get started by setting aside 10 minutes a day. It's less about intense workout routines and calorie tracking and more about self-care activities that keep you in shape. Even small things like a short walk or a few morning stretches help.

Balancing Fitness With Busy Schedules

Let's be real: some days, you barely have time to eat, let alone get in a workout. It's so much easier if your exercise of choice is something you actually look forward to, even if it's just a 10-minute pilates session or hopping on a treadmill while you binge a podcast. Try adding short bursts of activity into your daily routine—do a few squats while you wait for your coffee to brew or take the stairs instead of the elevator. Every bit counts. There's no rule that says you have to be at the gym for it to count as exercise.

Exercise Options

There are an insane amount of activities that qualify as exercise, but a few are classics for a reason.

- **Pilates:** Pilates is fantastic for building strength, stability, and flexibility without needing much space. Wall pilates is even a thing, and it's great if balance isn't one of your many talents. Plus, there are tons of free videos and apps with step-by-step tutorials.

- **Recreational Sports Leagues:** If you always had trophies everywhere as a kid, recreational sports leagues might be more your speed. If you're new to rec leagues, they're a great way to meet new friends. Look for beginner-friendly leagues in your area for sports like soccer, basketball, or frisbee.

- **Gyms/Fitness Classes:** Gyms are popular for a reason, and many of them have juice bars now. Most of them have free trial memberships, so you can see if it's a good fit first. If you prefer specialized classes, like dance, spin class, or boxing, there's a good chance that the gym offers them. And if not, it's a great place to snag a good recommendation.

- **Walking/Running/Biking:** This option is perfect if you need your exercise paired with your favorite music, podcast, or audiobook. It's free, flexible, and a great way to get some fresh air. Aim for 30 minutes, but odds are you'll lose track of time and just enjoy life.

Tips for Home Workouts

Maybe you're more of a homebody, or maybe you just do not care to be working out in front of a large group of strangers. Either way, your home can easily double as a personalized exercise space.

- **Find space:** A small space in your living room or bedroom is really all you need... think of how little room yoga mats take up? There are even leg exercises you can do on your bed while you log some social media scrolling time.

- **Use what you have:** If you want to get creative with makeshift weights by filling a backpack with books, by all means, go for it. Otherwise, you can focus on using your own body weight—like squats, lunges, planks, and push-ups. Some types of pilates even use walls and doorframes to your advantage.

- **Apps & videos:** If you need a little guidance, try fitness apps or YouTube videos. You'll most likely have to sit through some ads, but sometimes you can customize the routine to your body type and experience level.

- **Make it fun:** Dance workouts, VR fitness, or breaking out the Wii controllers. Just make sure you don't get a noise complaint if you live above anyone.

Safety Precautions

This obviously refers to making sure you don't end up needing to refer to the first aid section that's coming up. But there are also some people and situations to be mindful of. There is so much good in the world, but it pays to recognize the signs of the bad that goes with it. So, let's try to avoid both types of danger.

- **Listen to your body:** If something hurts, stop. It's doubtful that there's a Superbowl ring on the line, so it's better to let your body heal than keep going and make it worse. It never hurts to talk to a doctor if you're dealing with any kind of consistent pain.

- **Warm up & cool down:** Always take a few minutes to stretch and warm up before you start. Going into exercise "cold" puts unnecessary strain on your muscles. And a couple of stretches when you're done can help keep soreness to a minimum.

- **Stay hydrated:** Drink water before, during, and after your workout, especially if it's hot outside or you're sweating a lot. Sports drinks are great too, just don't rely on them alone.

- **Stay aware of your surroundings:** Any true crime fans are a step ahead. If you're running or walking outside, pick well-lit, busy areas and try to avoid wearing headphones at full blast—save a little hearing for warning noises.

- **Share your location:** If it's not possible to use the buddy system, let at least one person know where you are. Seriously, drop a pin.

- **Stranger danger:** Most of the time, meeting new people is amazing. But sadly, there are some instances of people with unsavory interests. Avoid putting yourself in situations that pull you away from the general public. Just because someone claims you've met before doesn't mean you owe them a ride anywhere. This doesn't mean you can't be kind; it means think before you act.

At the end of the day, find what you enjoy, be safe, and don't worry about being perfect. Fitness should add to your life, not make it more stressful.

Mental Health

This topic covers entirely too much, so there won't be helpful tips here. Everyone has a different version of mental health, so find what works for you. A friendly word of advice—not everything can be instantly solved with medications or deep breathing exercises. Sometimes, you just have to suck it up and work through tough situations. And that's also why a lot of people go to therapy, which is even better if it's covered by insurance. Onto to the next section.

Health Insurance

Hopefully, you have the option to hang out on your parents' health insurance until you turn 26. If not, there are a decent number of jobs—even part-time—that offer benefits. Insurance is up there on the list of very annoying things you deal with as an adult. It's confusing and expensive. But it's also a necessity.

Even if you're healthy now, unexpected things will happen. Without insurance, one hospital visit or ER trip could cost thousands of dollars—up to six figures for a major surgery. Insurance helps with stuff like that, plus yearly checkups.

Some key terms and what they mean:

- **Premium:** Your monthly payment for insurance coverage, essentially a membership fee.

- **Deductible:** The amount you pay each year before your insurance starts covering costs. Some policies cover preventive checkups without needing to meet the deductible. Check the fine print.

- **Copay:** A fixed amount you pay for doctor visits or prescriptions.

- **Coinsurance:** The percentage of costs you cover after meeting your deductible, typically 20-40%.

- **Network:** A list of doctors and facilities your plan covers at lower rates. Going "out of network" usually means higher costs.

- **Max out-of-pocket:** Your yearly cap on expenses before insurance covers everything at 100%.

Vision and Dental are almost always separate policies. Double-check if they're already part of your family's plan or if you'll need to look into that separately. There's no way to sugarcoat the complicated process of health insurance, but it's worth it in the long run.

First Aid

Having a basic understanding of first aid is just good knowledge. Don't try to fix a dislocated arm by yourself or anything, but knowing how to handle minor burns and cuts will help. The real trick is knowing when to ditch the first aid kit and go to an actual medical professional.

Basic First Aid Kit Necessities

Keep it somewhere permanent, like under the kitchen or bathroom sink, so you always know where it is. It's easier to buy a preassembled kit, but you can always build your own. Either way, these are foundation supplies:

- **Adhesive bandages:** For small cuts and scrapes—aim for a variety of sizes.

- **Antiseptic wipes and ointment:** To clean out cuts before the bandage goes on.

- **Gauze pads and medical tape:** These cover bigger wounds and help stop bleeding.

- **Tweezers:** Handy for splinters or removing small bits of debris.

- **Hydrocortisone cream:** Great for reducing itchiness from bites or rashes.

- **Pain relievers:** Like ibuprofen or acetaminophen for pain and fever.

- **Cold pack:** For bumps, bruises, or sprains.

- **Elastic bandage:** Helps support sprains or keep a cold pack in place.

Cuts, Scrapes, & Bites

For minor cuts and scrapes, a little cleaning and covering are usually all you need.

- **Clean the area:** Gently wash it with soap and water to get rid of dirt and germs.

- **Apply antiseptic:** Use an antiseptic wipe or ointment to prevent infection.

- **Cover with a bandage:** Grab a bandage of an appropriate size, and you're good to go.

For bug bites, hydrocortisone cream or an ice pack can help with itchiness. If a bite starts swelling a lot, changing colors, expanding in size, or causing any type of breathing/vision problems, get medical attention.

Burns

Everyone has that friend who swears by one 'amazing hack' for burns—mustard, ice, butter, you get the picture. Those aren't real and could actually cause more damage. If that friend comes near you with a condiment, tell them no. Here's what to do for real:

- **Cool the burn:** Don't stick your hand under ice-cold water because that can potentially irritate your nerves. Room temperature or slightly cool water running over the burn for a few minutes can reduce the pain.

- **Avoid home remedies:** Again, the 'hacks' can trap heat or lead to infection. Stick to burn ointment.

- **Cover with a sterile bandage:** Use a clean, non-stick bandage to protect the area. Healing time varies, so keep an eye on it and make sure it stays clean.

Allergic Reactions

Allergic reactions range from mildly annoying to serious. If you need an EpiPen, then you're already aware of the protocol—always have it nearby. If you know someone who requires an EpiPen, there are classes you can take to learn how to administer it correctly if you're ever in that situation. Other milder allergies can develop as you get older, so it's helpful knowing how to handle them.

- **Mild reactions:** If you notice a mild rash or itchiness, try an antihistamine like Benadryl and apply hydrocortisone cream. If the symptoms don't show any signs of leaving you alone, schedule a doctor's appointment.

- **Allergy testing:** Part of the fun aging process sometimes means being allergic to things you never used to be. Pets, strawberries, gluten... the options are irritatingly endless, so it doesn't hurt to get an allergy test every so often to stay ahead of things.

When To See a Doctor

Usually, the signs will be pretty clear that a bandage won't cut it. In the rare instances you aren't sure, don't risk it.

- **Deep cuts or heavy bleeding:** If a cut is gaping, won't stop bleeding, or you think it might need stitches, get it checked out.

- **Infected wounds:** If a wound is overly red, swollen, warm, or starts oozing, it may be infected, and you'll probably need prescription antibiotics.

- **Severe burns:** If a burn is bigger than three inches, your skin looks white or charred, or blisters immediately, go to the ER.

- **Persistent symptoms:** If you're dealing with an issue that doesn't improve after basic first aid—like the mild rash that is resisting Benadryl—it's time to see a doctor. Again, any kind of trouble controlling basic motor skills means an immediate trip to the emergency room.

Chapter 4:

Financial Literacy

Some people have a natural ability to keep track of all things financial, or at least they have family members who taught them well. Others have more of a "wing it" mentality. Wherever you fall on that scale, financial literacy is a tool for living your best life.

Money doesn't measure your worth, so get that out of your brain right now. Knowing how to manage what you have is what really matters. Even if you never have to worry about checking your bank account, budgeting will make sure it stays that way. Think about it—did Beyoncé or Oprah get where they are by spending whatever they wanted? No. They figured out how to spend, save, and invest like the bosses they are.

This is the part of adulting that future you will be so happy you learned now.

Credit Score

Your credit score is a number that tells lenders how likely you are to pay back borrowed money. It's based on a lot of things you probably don't have yet, like payment/credit history and debt amounts. A good score can help you get better rates on loans, which makes a big difference when you're making big purchases like a house.

Your credit score is likely going to be in the high 600s at this stage because you haven't had time to build that up. Small things like paying bills on time and avoiding unnecessary debt will naturally help. Credit cards are probably the first thing that comes to mind when raising your score, but we'll talk about why that's not always the best option later.

There are several trustworthy credit score apps, and your bank may even offer credit score tracking as a freebie.

Basic Budgeting Skills & Managing Expenses

It's unlikely that you don't already have a bank account. But maybe your parents have access to it, or you just want to see if there's a better option out there. A lot of banks or credit unions offer student or starter accounts with no fees. You can also look for sign-up bonuses if you set up direct deposit in a certain amount of days. That's easy free money if you meet the requirements.

Always, always, always remember to read the fine print, though. Find a bank you actually like and trust, not just any place that offers a good deal. Okay, let's get into the basics.

Savings

A separate savings account is a must—it's not always safe to rely on future you to leave a certain amount in checking every month. Look for one with good interest rates to earn a little extra. A lot of online banks offer higher rates than traditional banks, so it's worth shopping around. Some banks may try to talk about accounts like Roth IRAs, but basic checking and savings are just fine at this stage of life.

The best advice for a savings account is don't touch it! Unless it's an emergency situation, don't be tempted to pull a little bit out for a concert ticket or birthday present. Be realistic about what you can set aside for savings, and stick with your budget the best you can.

Budget Plan

If you're doing well financially, budgeting will keep you within your means and help that savings account get bigger. If you aren't bringing in a ton of cash, budgeting is borderline depressing. Why sugarcoat it?

But a budget will get you through money slumps without adding extra stress.

Start by calculating your monthly income, then list out your main expenses (rent, groceries, transportation, etc.). The goal is to spend less than you earn and try to save at least 10-20% each month. If the expenses are higher than your income, try to adjust what you can without starving yourself or moving into an unsafe living situation. Getting a loan may seem like a good option in that situation, but first see if there are any friends and family who can help until you get back on your feet.

Bonus Tips

- **Automate your savings:** Set up automatic transfers to your savings account each payday, even if it's only $5. Small amounts add up.

- **Track expenses:** Use an app to track your spending so you can see where your money's going in real-time. A lot of banks have this feature now.

- **Emergency fund:** Aim to save 3-6 months' worth of expenses as a buffer in case you're out of work or need a major car repair.

Credit Cards

Credit cards can be super helpful, but only if you know how to use them responsibly. They're great for emergencies and building up your credit score, but they're also a big reason why people are in debt.

Credit Card Interest and Debt

Credit cards are basically short-term loans. If you don't pay off the full balance each month, you'll get hit with interest on whatever you owe.

This is how credit card debt can build up faster than you'd think—credit card interest rates are typically around 15-25%.

The trick is treating it just like your bank account and not spending more than what you have. Pay off as much as you can each month to avoid racking up interest charges. Even a small balance accumulates more over time because of interest. It's best used for purchases you know you can pay off quickly.

Different Types of Credit Cards

If you do decide to get a card, you'll want one that fits your lifestyle and goals. And always read the fine print on interest rates, fees, and any rewards programs. Some companies are sneakier than others.

- **Standard credit cards:** These are the most basic cards with no fancy rewards or perks. They're usually targeted at people building credit, but make sure to compare interest rates.

- **Rewards cards:** Points, cashback, or miles for every dollar you spend. If you're someone who pays off the balance every month, these cards are a great way to get fun bonuses every now and then.

- **Secured credit cards:** Secured cards require a deposit upfront that acts as your credit limit. This option is a much safer way to build credit because you're essentially borrowing against your own money.

- **Student credit cards:** It's pretty obvious that these are designed for college students. Most of them come with lower limits and simpler reward programs—easier to manage if you're new to credit.

Credit Cards for Emergencies

Yes, credit cards have their risks, but they can also be a lifesaver in unexpected situations. Travel issues, cars breaking down, medical expenses—any kind of emergency. Having that lifeline means you don't need to scramble for cash when life throws a curveball. Just make sure you have a game plan for paying off within a reasonable amount of time.

Alternate Ways to Build Credit Without a Card

Maybe you know yourself well enough to realize that a credit card would lead to imminent financial disaster (many middle-aged people still haven't figured that out). Or maybe they just aren't your thing. Either way, there are other options:

- **Credit-builder loans:** Lots of banks and credit unions offer small loans specifically designed to help you build credit. You make payments each month, and once it's paid off, you get the funds back.

- **Authorized user:** You may not have a credit card, but someone you know probably does. Being added as an authorized user on their card (with their permission, of course) can help you build credit without managing your own account. Just make sure it's someone who pays on time.

Scholarships & Student Loans

College, trade schools, and skill-building courses aren't cheap. Whatever you're doing to grow your career will most likely mean dropping a large sum of money on some type of education. How you go about funding that depends on several things, but there are plenty of resources.

Scholarships

Scholarships don't have to be repaid, so they're an obvious first choice. Start by looking into scholarships your school offers, then branch out to national programs or local organizations. Eligibility requirements and deadlines will always be a thing, so be aware. Here are a few good starting options:

- **School guidance counselors:** Your high school guidance counselor can be a goldmine for local scholarships that don't always show up online. They usually have information on scholarships specific to your career field or college, plus they can walk you through the application process and write recommendation letters.

- **College financial aid offices:** Most schools have specific scholarships for incoming students, and they'll help you figure out if you qualify for any.

- **Community organizations and clubs:** Local groups like the Rotary Club, Lions Club, and Kiwanis offer scholarships. You might find some good opportunities with local businesses, so it's worth asking around.

- **Online scholarship platforms:** Several sites have massive databases of scholarships, and they'll match you with opportunities based on your profile. Just create an account, fill in your details, and browse the list.

- **Professional associations and unions:** A lot of industries and trade unions give scholarships to students interested in their field. If you're into journalism, look for scholarships from journalism associations. It's a great option if you already know what career path you're on.

Student Loans

If scholarships aren't an option, student loans can come in handy. Just check the interest rate and repayment terms carefully so you know exactly what you're signing up for.

- **Federal loans:** These are backed by the government and usually have lower interest rates and more flexible repayment options.

- **Private loans:** These are offered by banks and credit unions, so they tend to have higher interest rates. They're best for filling in gaps if federal aid isn't enough.

- **Parent PLUS loans:** These are federal loans your parents can take out on your behalf, often with higher borrowing limits but also higher interest rates. It's worth considering how this will affect your overall relationship, too.

Managing Debt After College

A large percentage of the population is paying off school debt. Hopefully, if you become part of this group, you'll get a really low interest rate, but there are still many repayment options to take advantage of. Here are a few common ones:

- **Income-driven repayment plans:** These adjust your monthly payments based on your income, which is extra helpful if your monthly income fluctuates.

- **Teacher loan forgiveness:** If you go into teaching, you may qualify for partial loan forgiveness after a certain number of years. Check the guidelines for your area.

- **Public service loan forgiveness (PSLF):** If you work in public service, you might qualify for forgiveness after 10 years of payments. That sounds like much longer than it really is, trust me.

Pro tip: If you can't pay, get ahead of the situation. Call your loan provider and let them know what's going on. Sometimes, they'll help you by deferring the loan due to personal difficulties or adjusting your payment amount.

Chapter 5:

Taxes & Civic Knowledge

Alright, these topics might not be what you chat about at brunch, but they're important. You can't get out of things like filing taxes and mandatory laws, so it's best to know what you're in for. It's really not as daunting as it seems, but speaking of daunting, we'll start with taxes.

Paying Taxes

Taxes can be overwhelming and they're pretty much always irritating, but it's good to know what's coming out of your paycheck and why. The main types of taxes you'll notice:

- **Income tax:** The big one. This is the tax on your earnings and varies based on how much you make and what your tax bracket is. We'll get more into filing income taxes in the next section.

- **Sales tax:** You pay this every time you buy something. The rate depends on where you live, and it's usually added to the price of goods and services.

- **Property tax:** If you own property, like a house, land, or vehicle, you'll pay property taxes based on the value of that property. What you pay usually supports local schools, roads, and services.

- **Social Security and Medicare (Payroll Taxes):** These are deductions taken from your paycheck to fund Social Security and Medicare programs, which go toward retirement and healthcare benefits.

- **Excise taxes:** Think "extra fees" on things like gasoline, cigarettes, or alcohol. It's typically included in the price and goes toward specific government projects.

All these taxes support different areas of government spending, but income tax is the one you'll deal with the most—and the one you'll file every year. And now for how that process works.

Tax Filing

Filing taxes is one of the more tedious adulting tasks, especially if you end up owing money instead of getting a refund. Basically, you're reporting your income to the IRS, and there are different ways to file. The big mistakes to avoid are not filing at all or filing late, both of which lead to pretty large penalties.

Common Types of Tax Forms

- **W-2 Form:** If you have a traditional job, your employer will send you a W-2 showing your earnings and how much tax was withheld. You'll need this to file, and it's usually sent out by January 31.

- **1099 Form:** Freelancers, contractors, or anyone with "side gig" income will likely receive a 1099 form. It shows income from work where taxes weren't withheld, which means you might owe extra on that amount.

- **1040 Form:** This is the main form you use to file your individual income tax return. You'll enter your income, deductions, and credits to calculate how much tax you owe or how much you'll get back as a refund.

- **1098-T Form:** If you're a student, this shows tuition and other school-related expenses. It helps you claim education credits to reduce your tax bill if you qualify.

- **1098-E Form:** If you're paying off student loans, this form reports interest paid on those loans, which you may be able to deduct. It's a small but helpful deduction if you qualify.

How to File

Most people file as "Single" (not married) or "Married Filing Jointly," but there are other types like "Married Filing Separately" and "Head of Household." Whatever you choose impacts your tax rate and potential deductions. It could also affect your decision on how you file, but these are the most popular:

- **Using tax software:** Things like TurboTax or H&R Block can walk you through the filing process step by step. They're very convenient, but they've been known to throw in extra forms or questions to make the process look complicated, so you'll upgrade to a paid version. If you have a simple tax situation, you might be fine with the free or basic options.

- **Hiring an accountant:** If your finances are complex or you're just unsure, hiring an accountant is a great option. They know all the ins and outs of how to maximize deductions and avoid any filing mistakes. Plus, you'll have an accountant every year who's already familiar with your situation.

Should You Pay Yearly or Quarterly?

Most people pay taxes once a year, but if you're self-employed or run a business, you'll likely want to pay quarterly.

- **Yearly filing (most common):** If you're an employee, your employer automatically withholds taxes from each paycheck, so you just file a return once a year to square everything up with the IRS. Most of the time, you won't owe.

- **Quarterly payments (self-employed):** If you're self-employed, you're responsible for withholding your own taxes. Making estimated tax payments every three months helps spread out the tax load and keeps you from facing a massive bill at the end of the year, which is never a fun surprise.

Voting Registration

Voting is your right, but it's also your choice. There will always be pressure about voting no matter how old you are, but the only influence that matters right now is your own. Vote or don't vote. Either way, it's good to know you have a say in issues that matter to you. It also doesn't hurt to know how the process works if you decide to be election-ready.

Step 1: Know the Basics

Most people are eligible to vote at 18, but the requirements can always vary depending on where you live. Your state's election website should have the guidelines and residency requirements.

Step 2: Registering to Vote

- **Online:** This is the go-to voter registration option for obvious reasons. You'll need a form of ID, like a driver's license or social security number, and an address.

- **Mail:** You can download a voter registration form, fill it out, and send it to your local election office. Just in case the internet is down forever, I suppose.

- **In-person:** Almost as unlikely as mailing in your registration, the DMV, public assistance offices, and election offices offer in-person registration. You never know.

Step 3: Current Registration

If you move, change your name, or switch states, you'll need to update your registration. You can usually update this pretty quickly online.

Step 4: Voting Options

- In-person on Election Day.
- Early Voting (voting in person before Election Day).
- Absentee Voting (voting by mail, usually for students or anyone who can't make it to their polling place).

Step 5: Get Informed

If you decide to hit the polls, keep an eye out for upcoming elections and research candidates or issues on the ballot. Knowledge is key here.

Jury Duty

Definitely not the most glamorous part of adulting, but it comes with the territory. Depending on the case, it's a pretty interesting experience once you're there. Full disclosure: it can also be mind-numbingly boring. Here's what you need to know:

What is Jury Duty and How Do You Get Chosen?

Citizens get randomly selected to serve as jurors in a trial. They listen to all the evidence presented in a case, consider the facts, and then help decide whether the defendant is guilty or not guilty (in criminal cases) or decide the outcome in civil cases (like a lawsuit). The random selection for jury duty comes from a pool of registered voters, driver's license holders, or people with state-issued IDs. Most people are only called once in a while, and some people never get called.

What Happens After You Get Summoned?

You'll receive a jury duty notice in the mail with the date, time, and location of your potential jury service. Here's what to expect after that:

- **Check the dates:** The notice will give you instructions on whether you need to show up right away or if you can call in the night before to see if they actually need you. Sometimes, not everyone is needed for every trial, so you might not have to appear.

- **Go to the court:** If you are required, you'll need to show up at the courthouse at the specified time. Bring your jury summons, photo ID, and any other requested documents.

- **Jury selection (Voir Dire):** When you get there, you'll be put in a group of potential jurors. Both attorneys involved in the trial will ask questions to see if you're a good fit for that particular case. If they think you're biased or have a conflict of interest, you could be dismissed. This part is called "voir dire," and it's normal to feel like you're on the spot—it's just part of making sure the trial is fair.

- **Serving on the jury:** If you're selected, you'll sit through the trial, hear both sides of the case, and decide on a verdict with the rest of the jury.

Is There a Way to Get Out of Jury Duty?

It depends. There are some valid reasons you can be excused, but just ignoring a jury duty summons can lead to fines or legal consequences. It's best to stick with the valid reasons if they apply to you:

- **Health issues:** You can provide a doctor's note to be excused if you're physically or mentally unable to serve.

- **Financial hardship:** If serving on a jury would seriously screw up your income (especially if you're self-employed or don't get paid while on duty), you might be excused.

- **Pre-existing commitments:** If you have a pre-planned event, like a wedding or a work obligation, you may be able to at least postpone your jury duty.

- **Conflicts of interest:** If you know one of the parties involved in the case or have a strong opinion about the trial, you might be excused during voir dire.

Other Things to Know

Does Jury Duty Pay?

The pay for jury duty varies by location, but it's generally not a lot. Some employers still pay you while you're serving, but don't bank on that. You may get a small stipend or reimbursement for travel expenses.

How Long Does It Last?

Jury duty typically lasts for a day or two, but there's a chance you could get selected for a longer trial. Those can last anywhere from a few days to several weeks. Always check your summons for specifics.

What Happens After the Verdict?

After the trial ends and a verdict is reached, you're free to go back to your normal routine. Depending on the case, there might be media coverage, so keep in mind that you're expected to maintain confidentiality during the trial.

Selective Service

The Selective Service is basically a list the U.S. government keeps of eligible males for potential military drafts. Registration is required for all males once they turn 18. At the time of writing, there's a chance registration might become automatic in the future. For now, let's assume it's on you to register within 30 days of your 18th birthday.

Registration is easy—go to the Selective Service System website, enter your information, and you're set. These are the most common FAQs for Selective Service:

- "What if I miss the 30-day deadline?"
    - No worries if you miss the first month—you can still register any time before you turn 26. But it's better to get it done sooner rather than later because waiting can cause delays in benefits or getting a security clearance.

- "What if I'm a non-citizen?"
    - Most non-citizen males, even without documentation, are required to register within 30 days of their 18th birthday. There are some exemptions like student visas, active military, or permanent residents of other countries. Missing the deadline can affect future visa or citizenship opportunities, so make sure to check if you need to register.

- "Will I definitely be drafted if there's a war?"
    - Not necessarily. Registering just puts your name on a list; it doesn't mean you're automatically headed off to basic training. If a draft ever happened, you'd still have options for deferments based on student status, hardship, or other legitimate reasons. There's less reliance on ground combat roles than there has been in the past.

- "What if I identify as non-binary or trans?"
    - While the rules haven't fully adapted to include non-binary or transgender identities (at the time of writing), it currently says anyone assigned male at birth who hasn't undergone full gender reassignment surgery still has to register.

Chapter 6:

Emergency Preparedness

Emergency preparedness probably makes you think of the movies and that cow getting sucked up into a tornado. In all fairness, weather is one of the main reasons for having supplies handy. A bag filled with the essentials will make a world of difference if dangerous weather decides to throw you a curveball.

There is another side of being prepared that helps in other scenarios that will hopefully never happen to you. Yes, house fires are a possibility. But what if you need to leave your home quickly because of *someone*, not *something*? The faster you can get yourself away from risky situations, the better. So, being ready for emergencies is about more than knowing where the flashlight is. It's about adding an extra layer of security for all types of unpredictable life events.

Go-Bag Essentials

A go-bag is exactly what it sounds like—a grab-and-go emergency kit. Ideally, you'll want a bag that's waterproof, but don't worry if it's not. Aim for something with straps, like a backpack or duffel bag that you can wear crossbody-style.

Where you keep your go-bag depends heavily on your lifestyle. Since your ID won't live in this bag, keeping it near your wallet and keys isn't a bad idea.

What to Include:

- Change of clothes (two if there's room, and update for seasons)
- Basic hygiene items
- Some non-perishable food and a few bottles of water
- Phone charger (a solar-powered one is a good backup to have)
- Flashlight with extra batteries
- Small first-aid kit
- Multi-tool
- Some cash (best not to tell anyone it's in there)
- Any medications you take regularly
- Optional: Important documents (like insurance info in a waterproof pouch)

Pets:

Go for a small bag that can be clipped onto your own go-bag. That way, you'll be able to grab everything at once, including your pet. For cats or other small critters, you can just use a cat carrier. Here are the pet basics:

- Leash/collar
- Small amount of food
- Any medications
- Collapsible water bowl
- Blanket or toy (if there's room)

Weather-Related Emergencies

Weather can hit hard and fast, and each event has its own set of precautions. You probably know what your area is known for, so be prepared.

- **Tornado:** Know where the safest room is (ideally a basement or interior room with no windows). Keep a battery-powered radio on hand to stay updated in case the phone signals go down.

- **Flood:** Move valuables to higher ground, stay updated on alerts, and have an evacuation plan. Don't walk or drive through floodwaters even if it seems okay—they can be way deeper and more dangerous than they look. It's not easy fighting a flood current, so just avoid them.

- **Hurricane:** Stock up on non-perishable food, water, and other essentials well in advance. Fill the tub so you have a supply of water for hygiene and fill a bucket for flushing the toilet. Board up windows if you need to, and stay in a safe, windowless room. If you see an evacuation advisory, get out of there.

- **Snowstorm:** Winter storms can knock out power and water. In 2021, large parts of Texas didn't have power for weeks. Be ready with warm blankets, extra food and water, and make sure your phone is fully charged. If you have a fireplace or space heater, use it safely.

Fire

After Chapter 2, you know to have extinguishers and fire blankets on hand, but fires can start and spread quickly through no fault of your own. Normally, an emergency situation means calling 911 immediately. In a fire, getting out safely first is often more important.

- **Put on shoes:** Yes, shoes again. Beyond broken glass and debris on the floor, burnt feet make it very hard to walk. Give yourself a better chance of getting out safely.

- **If you can't locate the fire:** In some cases, you'll be surrounded by smoke and not know where the source is. Stay low, cover your mouth and nose, and check your exits for fire before running through. Once you're out, you can call for help.

- **If exits are blocked:** Stay low to the ground and do your best to avoid smoke and heat. Close doors between you and the fire if you can, and use cloth items to block smoke from entering. If you're on a higher floor, open a window if you can. Stay on the phone with 911 as long as possible and tell them exactly where you're located inside.

Blackout

Blackouts can happen for a range of reasons, from bad weather to power grid overloads. They usually last from a few minutes to several hours, but in rare cases, they can stretch for days. They're much more common in bigger cities, so keep that in mind if you're new to areas like that.

If you get stuck driving when a blackout hits, treat every intersection like a four-way stop and be extra wary of pedestrians. Do not stop until you get somewhere safe that's closest to you—friends, parents, school, wherever it is. Don't stop for strangers, either.

Basic Tips & Safety:

- Keep flashlights (be careful with candles since they're a fire risk).

- Avoid opening the fridge/freezer to keep food cool.

- If it's hot out, stay hydrated and avoid excessive effort.

- If it's cold, get warm blankets and layer up.

- Be super cautious about answering your door.

- On that note, keep all doors and windows locked.

Domestic Emergency

If you're in a situation that feels unsafe because of someone's behavior or you're afraid of intruders, it's important to have a plan. It's always okay to ask for help if you're in an unsafe living environment. Always!

This isn't something that comes with black-and-white rules, but there are small things you can do.

- **Signs to watch for:** Extreme mood swings, sudden anger or aggression, and any signs of controlling or threatening behavior can be early indicators of escalating danger.

- **Know where to go:** Decide on a safe place to go in advance, like a friend's house, family, or a local shelter. Keep an emergency contact who you can alert quickly if needed—drop a pin.

- **Call for help:** If you aren't able to leave, try to get somewhere secure with a locked door and call 911. The steps after that are up to you, but there are many, many supportive resources to help. Physical and mental abuse is not okay, and you deserve better.

Basic Survival Skills

Your idea of being outdoorsy might be drinking coffee on a patio. That's totally fine, but having a few basic survival skills can be life-saving in an emergency.

- **First aid certified:** Knowing basic first aid can help you stabilize an injury until help gets there. Courses are widely available and well worth the time.

- **Fire safety:** Know how to start a fire safely and how to put one out. This is especially useful in case you're somewhere without power and need to stay warm.

- **Water purification:** Water will always be an emergency, so why not learn how to purify it—boiling, using tablets, or filters.

- **Shelter-making:** Knowing how to set up a basic shelter really comes in handy if you're caught in a weather emergency outside.

- **Navigation:** Basic map reading and compass skills are helpful if you need to navigate without GPS. Even if the grid doesn't go down, your phone could die.

- **Extras:** Skills like knot-tying or basic foraging can be useful if you ever find yourself stuck in the wilderness. There are several types of berries and fungi that will make you sick or even kill you if you eat them.

Bonus Emergency Preparedness Kits

No one's saying you need to build a full bunker, but keeping a few extra essentials at home and in your car can help you feel extra prepared.

Home Kit:

- A few days' worth of food and water.
- Flashlights and lanterns with extra batteries.
- Basic tool kit and first aid.
- Medications and basic pain relievers.
- Extra clothes and blankets.
- Optional: Books, games, and other non-electronic entertainment.

Car Kit:

- Flares
- Jumper cables
- Spare tire and jack
- Basic first-aid kit
- Blankets
- Flashlight
- Ice scraper and shovel (for colder areas)
- Water and non-perishable snacks (switch these out regularly)

Chapter 7:

Transportation & Travel

Planes, trains, and automobiles. There are a lot of ways to get from point A to point B, so we might as well go over all of them. This obviously depends heavily on where you live and how many places you need to go every day.

Public Transportation

In some places (looking at you, Japan), public transportation runs with clockwork precision. Unfortunately, most of the US is not known for that. Give yourself some extra wiggle room if you're relying on certain types of public transportation. Each one has its pros and cons.

Bus

- **Pros:**
    - Affordable and widely available, especially in urban and suburban areas.
    - Great for short-distance travel and stops frequently, so there's usually a bus stop near where you need to go.
    - Often has discounted fares for students, seniors, and frequent riders.
- **Cons:**
    - Expect them to be slow, especially during rush hour.

- Unreliable schedules mean you might wait a bit longer than expected.
- Crowded buses are pretty uncomfortable.

Train/Trolley

- **Pros:**
  - Reliable and usually faster than buses for medium to long distances.
  - You're way less affected by road traffic.
  - Tends to run on a predictable schedule, which makes planning easier.
- **Cons:**
  - Limited routes compared to buses, so you might need another way to get to and from the station.
  - Some trains are standing-room only during peak hours.
  - Ticket prices can vary, and some lines are pricier than others.

Subway

- **Pros:**
  - Fastest option in busy urban areas by far.
  - Frequent stops mean you can usually find a station within walking distance of key spots.
  - Runs frequently, so they're very convenient for spontaneous travel.

- **Cons:**
    - Pretty confusing to navigate if you're new to the system or the city.
    - Super crowded during rush hour with limited seating.
    - Subways aren't available in all cities, so if your area doesn't have one, you're out of luck.

Ferry

- **Pros:**
    - A scenic route and fresh air (a definite plus if you're tired of crowded buses and trains).
    - Useful for cities with water channels, like New York or Seattle.
    - Some have food and drink options on board, so that's a bonus.
- **Cons:**
    - Not ideal if you're in a hurry; ferries have slower speeds and less frequent schedules.
    - Limited routes since they're specific to coastal or riverside cities.
    - The weather can affect them, which might delay or cancel trips.

Uber/Lyft

- **Pros:**
    - Convenient and available pretty much anywhere.
    - Door-to-door service, which is especially helpful if you're carrying a lot or going somewhere that's hard to reach by public transit.
    - Flexible timing, so you don't have to work around a schedule or wait at a stop.
- **Cons:**
    - Price can add up fast, especially during surge pricing periods or holidays.
    - Limited availability in rural areas or during peak demand.
    - You're very reliant on a total stranger.

e-scooters

- **Pros:**
    - Super convenient for short trips, especially in cities where they're parked and ready to rent all over.
    - Fun and fast.
    - Usually cheaper than rideshares.
- **Cons:**
    - Not ideal for gross weather days.

- They're a bit unsafe if there's no designated bike lane (always bring a helmet!).
- Limited battery life and speed, so they're best for short trips only.

Time management

Always check schedules in advance and track live updates if available. Expect delays, especially with buses and subways. Arriving late is no fun, so plan for a buffer just in case.

Driving

There are countless areas where public transportation isn't a thing or is just flat-out terrible. In those scenarios, you're most likely relying on a car. It should go without saying to stay away from creepy unlit parking lots and garages. Hard pass. Here's a rundown of the driving basics that you probably already know, but just in case.

Insurance & Registration

Don't drive a car that's not insured and registered. It will cause you so much more trouble in the long run. Keep these documents updated in case you're ever in an accident.

What to Keep in the Glove Box & Trunk

Insurance card, registration, and an emergency contact list. This is not a must, but extra napkins in the glovebox will come in handy. In the trunk, keep a spare tire, jack, jumper cables, and a basic first aid kit (the stuff we just talked about in Chapter 6).

Regular Tune-Ups

Schedule oil changes, check tire pressure, and make sure your lights and wipers are functioning. Keeping up with oil changes is a lot cheaper than the damage that comes from ignoring them. Also, have you ever been driving with only one windshield wiper? Zero stars, don't recommend.

If Your Car Breaks Down or Wrecks

First, try to stay calm, even though it's a scary situation. Turn on your hazard lights immediately and move to a safe area if possible. If you have roadside assistance, give them a call. If not, call someone who can come help you. Knowing how to change a tire is a very helpful skill (YouTube has plenty of tutorials). Hopefully, everyone is okay in the case of a wreck. Exchange information with the other driver(s) involved and go from there.

Pro tip: watch some videos and ask a knowledgeable buddy for some instruction and practice on changing a tire or correctly attaching jumper cables before an emergency happens. Your future stranded self will be SO glad you did!

Flying & Travel

Flying can be a little intimidating, especially if it's your first time, but it's also one of the fastest ways to travel long distances. There are also a lot of details—booking the right flight, baggage restrictions, not to mention international travel. But vacations are the best, so here we go.

Booking Your Flight

- Check prices on multiple platforms to scope out the best deal.

- Book early if you can—flights tend to be cheaper the farther out you book, and tickets are usually higher if you buy close to your departure date.

- Direct flights are typically more expensive, but you avoid the dreaded layover. Flights with layovers might lower the cost, but they can also add extra hours and stress to your trip.

Packing Essentials

- Carry-on bags are usually free with most airlines, so try to pack light to avoid extra baggage fees. Trust me... when deciding what clothes to take, if you don't love it and feel great in it, don't bother. You won't wear it on your trip. Try outfits on to make the final decisions. Nothing is worse than realizing once you are on the other side of the ocean that the outfit you envisioned actually isn't so cute on! If you can't get it all in your carry-on, mark your checked baggage really well so you can spot it more easily. A small tracking tag wouldn't hurt either, in case your luggage gets lost.

- At the time of writing, the 3-1-1 rule for liquids still applies: each item should be 3.4 ounces or less, and all fit in a 1-quart bag with only 1 bag per passenger.

- Keep essentials (ID, boarding pass, wallet, phone, chargers, and any meds) in an easy-to-reach spot in the bag you'll take on the plane with you. This also goes for lithium batteries and e-cigarettes. These are a no-no in checked baggage, so you'll need to keep them with you during the flight.

Airport Security

- A good rule of thumb is getting to the airport at least 2 hours early for domestic flights and 3 hours early for international—security lines can be intense.

- Wear shoes that are easy to slip on and off and avoid lots of metal jewelry or accessories to speed up the security screening process.

- Keep your electronics and 3-1-1 liquid bag easily accessible because they'll need to go in a separate bin for scanning.

Boarding Tips

- Airlines typically board by group, so listen carefully to announcements or check your boarding pass for your group number.

- If you're carrying on luggage, get in line early enough to snag overhead bin space. Otherwise, be ready to gate-check your bag if the bins fill up.

- You don't have to be this person, but you can bring travel-size sanitizing wipes for your tray table and armrests. Some airlines provide them, but some don't.

In-Flight Comfort

- Dress in layers—airplane cabins can range from artic to sauna with rarely a good middle ground.

- Bring snacks and a water bottle (fill it up after security) since airplane food options can be pricey and limited.

- Download books, movies, or games before you board to keep yourself occupied, especially on long flights. And a travel neck pillow is never a bad option.

Arrival & Baggage Claim

- If you checked a bag, follow signs to the baggage claim area. Keep your baggage claim ticket (usually given at check-in) handy in case there are any mix-ups.

- For international flights, you'll need to go through customs and may have to show your passport again, so have it ready.

- Double-check that you have everything before leaving the airport. It's so easy to forget small things after a long flight.

Safety & Courtesy tips

Rude people exist everywhere, and it seems like public transportation draws them in even more. But that doesn't mean you have to be one of them. Staying safe is the most important priority, though.

Politeness on Transit

Be aware of your surroundings. Offer a seat if someone needs it, keep the noise down, and give space to other passengers. Basically, don't sit right next to someone when there are plenty of open seats, and don't blast TikTok videos. Headphones and spatial awareness are the name of the game here.

Driving Courtesy

Road rage isn't worth it whether you're the rager or being raged at. People are unpredictable, so stay in your lane and try to go about your day. Aside from following basic traffic and driving rules, this is one area where being 'polite' isn't always safe. Road rules come before being nice. If the light is green, but you stop to let someone cut in—that could actually cause an accident. Keep details like that in mind and ignore the people who are angry for no reason.

Staying Safe on Public Transport & Walking

Keep your belongings close to you, stay in well-lit areas at night, and avoid distractions (like your phone) when walking near traffic. Trust your instincts! Don't hesitate to move to a busier area if you feel uncomfortable. This has been said multiple times—share your location with friends and family. Always.

Travel Safety

Keep copies of important documents in a secure spot, don't flash large amounts of cash, and stay aware of your surroundings. Research your area as thoroughly as you can before you get there, including local laws. Let people at home know your travel itinerary.

Chapter 8:

Relationships & Communication

Social media, new roommates, questionable bosses—all of these things involve knowing when and how to speak up and set boundaries. But since communication differs drastically for everyone in every situation, we're not getting into niche details. We're focusing on basic tips that can be adjusted to your life. There is one hard and fast rule: sometimes good communication and boundary setting won't do the trick. In that case, it might be best to move on from that particular situation. Anyway, back to advice for reasonable scenarios.

Social Media

Privacy

Not *everything* needs to be public. We're in the age of tech where people can probably find information if they want to. But you can make it harder for them, at least. Keep an eye on your friend/follower lists, use privacy settings, and keep personal information protected as best you can. Report anything creepy or scammy. It's also a good idea to avoid posting anything that shows your current location. Anything that makes it obvious where you are, like in front of an iconic building or landmark, post it after you've left and not while you are still there. You don't want unsavory people knowing where to find you or even when your home is unoccupied.

Online Communication

You're not obligated to respond instantly or at all! If your group gets annoyed because you have a habit of ghosting them, that's on you. But anyone who starts arguments unnecessarily, ask yourself if it's worth engaging. Sometimes, it's best to step away.

Digital Balance

Screen time can have some unfortunate effects. Keep an eye on how it impacts your mood. If your mental health takes a dip, maybe put the phone down for a while.

Censorship

Freedom of speech is a basic right. Being able to share thoughts and opinions is important. Keep in mind that everything you share is out there forever, even if you delete it. It's on you to monitor what you put online. Just a reminder to think before you post.

Roommates

Set Boundaries Early On

Set up a time to talk about cleaning schedules, personal vs. shared items, quiet hours, and when you can have people over. Getting on the same page from the start makes everything easier. It also prevents loud guests from showing up at 2 AM (hopefully).

Addressing Conflicts

It's tempting to go straight for passive-aggressive, but calm will usually work better. Try not to let issues pile up and talk about them (respectfully) when they happen. Compromise where possible to keep the peace.

Privacy

Everyone needs personal space. Stay out of theirs, and they'll stay out of yours, which should be the general vibe. If someone is crossing a line, they may not even realize it, so just say something nicely. If all else fails, put a lock on your bedroom door.

Friends & Family

Setting Expectations

Balancing your social time with personal downtime helps a lot. Burnout usually happens from ignoring your limits and over-committing. It's okay to set boundaries with people based on how much time you can spend with them—even family.

Difficult Conversations

New independence, new lifestyle, new opinions—whatever it is, family and friends might not understand it. Be direct and clear, and hope for the best. That's all you can really do.

Mental Health

Keep an eye on toxic patterns like gaslighting and subtle put-downs all the time. It's okay to say no without feeling guilty if something doesn't feel right. At the very least, you can try to limit your time around certain people without missing out on things like family holidays.

Coworkers & Bosses

Professional Boundaries

Every work environment is different, but it's always good to have some ground rules in place. Make sure your team knows when you're offline—most jobs don't require an immediate response at all hours of the day and night. Be careful what kind of language you use. And avoid oversharing, even if it seems like a tight-knit group.

Say What You Need

If you need time off or feel overwhelmed with the tasks on your plate, don't hesitate to speak up in a professional way. There's no guarantee you'll get the time off or help, but you don't know if you don't try.

Handling Workplace Conflicts

If it's something small, like someone keeps taking your pens, try calmly asking them to stop. If things get serious, go to HR or a manager you trust for help. This is a good example of how sometimes there's only so much you can do. If you're in a bad work environment, look into other employment options or maybe even consider a career change.

Romantic Relationships

Early Boundaries

Dating is a whole different ball game now, but the basic rules are still the same. Especially this one: If they don't like or respect the "weird" things about you, that's probably not your person. It's not like you have to give them a manual of all of your quirks but set your boundaries early. It's a time saver.

Conflict

Do you fight a lot? Are there easy compromises, or do you end up 'losing'? Do you avoid certain topics or activities to avoid conflict? Just food for thought. Walking on eggshells around your partner all the time isn't a very fun way to live.

Consent & Comfort

This one is a no-brainer. Let them know if a line has been crossed. If they respect that, wonderful. If not, that's a no-go.

Neighbors

Being Friendly

You don't have to love them, but it's usually easier to be friendly. A simple wave or a nod when you see them goes a long way. If the creep factor is a little too high, keep tabs on things and maybe avoid crossing paths if possible.

Issues

With problems like noise complaints or cars parked where they shouldn't be, you can start by asking them nicely to stop whatever is happening. The next step is contacting management if that's an option or calling the non-emergency line. Your choice here also depends on whether you're worried about any kind of retaliation, but hopefully that's not the case.

Shared Spaces

Follow the building or HOA rules and clean up after yourself in any common areas. Be friendly but walk the line between being a good neighbor and overly intrusive.

Setting Boundaries With Yourself

Knowing Your Limits

This circles back to not overcommitting even if you feel like you have to. Sure, saying no will have repercussions sometimes. But you can't do much for anyone else if you're running on empty.

Healthy Routines

There's a lot more about this in Chapter 1, but just for a reminder—balance productivity with downtime. Throw in some vegetables and a little exercise every now and then.

Self-Care

It's okay to take breaks. Literally everyone needs a break sometimes. Just make sure you're not using small stressors as an excuse to put off actual responsibilities.

Chapter 9:

Career Skills

Building a career is a lot different than it used to be. Depending on your skill set and interests, you can go the more traditional college or trade school route or start your own business. Whichever path you're heading down, it's still good to know how to present yourself, network, and keep a decent professional profile. Even if you plan on being an entrepreneur, it's almost a guarantee you'll need a resume or portfolio at some point. May as well create one.

Resume & Portfolio

Crafting Your Resume

If you're just starting out, focus on transferable skills that apply to a wide range of roles (communication, problem-solving, organization, you get it). If things look a little too sparse, add any certificates, training courses, extracurriculars, future school goals, or anything relevant that shows you're working toward that specific career goal.

Choosing the Right Resume Style

This is very industry-dependent. Some want colorful templates, others want a photo, and a few still want a black-and-white one-pager. There are tons of free templates for every style. Do a little research and figure out what your job role looks like the most. You'll get an overwhelming amount of tips, so don't stress over all of them.

Super important tip: Check. Your. Grammar. Typos will almost always get your resume tossed in the 'No' pile. Have a friend look it over as well... an extra pair of eyes reading it over for mistakes is never a bad idea!

Tailoring for Each Role

This is time-consuming, and honestly, it's annoying. But it does help. Adjust your resume to match each job description, even if it's just using the same keywords from the listing. It helps prove you're willing to put in extra effort.

Cover Letters

It's generally best to keep things concise and genuine. A lot of employers are more interested in how your skills will help their team or project. They'll see your work history on the actual resume, so use the cover letter as a chance to stand out instead of regurgitating duplicate information.

Portfolio

Some industries still want a tangible portfolio, but you should be all set with a snazzy digital option. Research what the trends are for online portfolios and highlight all the lovely work you've done. Creative industries tend to have a specific spot to paste your portfolio link—and sometimes, it's non-negotiable.

Professional Online Profiles

LinkedIn Basics

LinkedIn is a must-have for most jobs. Use a professional picture—no other people, no crazy backgrounds, no distracting outfits. It's okay if you don't have a work history; just focus on adding skills and school information.

P.S. Retail and service industry jobs have a ton of transferable skills. Add them! From there, it's up to you how active you want to be.

Showcasing Your Skills

Same deal as the resume. Add any projects, certifications, and relevant interests that fit with your career goals. Everyone has to start somewhere, so don't worry about things seeming 'small.'

Networking Do's & Don'ts

It's absolutely okay to reach out to potential connections, clients, or employers. As long as you're not spamming people with messages, that's the entire point of LinkedIn. On the other side of this coin, you'll end up with a lot of robotic messages and offers that have nothing to do with your skillset. It's not always necessary to respond to each one—use your judgment.

Privacy & Professionalism

Keep your accounts private if you'd rather separate your professional and personal life. You can also adjust your LinkedIn settings to manage who sees what on your profile. Circling back to Chapter 7, be mindful of what you share; everything reflects on your professional image.

Job Searching Strategies

Job Boards & Platforms

LinkedIn is a good starting point for job searching. You can also Google 'Jobs hiring in (insert industry).' Use keywords, filter by location, and specify whether you're looking for remote, hybrid, or in-person work to help narrow down your search.

Pro tip: Easy Apply buttons aren't effective. Go to the actual company website and apply for the job that way. Your odds go way up. It can take up to 45 days to fill any given role in any industry, so be ready for lengthy wait times. It's also rare to hear back from every job you apply to—stay motivated because it can get a little disheartening sometimes.

Freelancing Platforms

The gig economy is growing astronomically, and there are quite a few reputable platforms where you can create a profile and pick up one-off projects. If you like to write, you can build your portfolio through freelance gigs. Just keep a few things in mind for these types of platforms:

- You'll probably have to start with low-paying projects.

- There's a higher chance of wishy-washy clients when you're first starting out.

- They take a decent percentage of your earnings.

- You won't always like the finished product.

Some of those seem obvious, but freelancing has its own set of challenges because everything falls on you. The freedom is great, but be ready for the potential obstacles that come with it.

Scam Awareness

Beware of job postings that promise huge salaries for little work or ask for upfront fees. Real jobs won't ask for your bank information until after you're hired. A few other red flags:

- Downloading a specific app just to interview.
- The company site feels too new or just 'off.'
- They want to send you a check to buy equipment.
- The email address doesn't match the company.
- There's never a video or phone interview.
- They want your personal information before onboarding.
- They never send you an official job offer.

Interview Tips

Preparation Basics

- **Research the company:** Look up the company's website, recent news, and any social media profiles. Essentially, you want to learn their values, goals, and culture. They'll be able to tell that you put in work.
- **"Tell Me About Yourself":** This question will always come up, and it's one of the easiest things to stumble over. Write down a short overview of yourself so you sound confident and don't end up rambling—two to three minutes is usually a good length. Start with where you live (really only applies to remote jobs), then mention pets, one hobby/interest/recent event, a

short description of your work history/skills, and end on a brief note about any future ambitions.

- **Prepare a few stories:** Think of three or four specific examples from past jobs, school projects, or volunteer work that show off your strengths. You'll most definitely be asked about your teamwork, problem-solving, or leadership skills, so having these stories ready will help. Again, avoid rambling and keep things concise. And make sure you don't talk trash about past bosses or coworkers—unintentionally or not.

Dress Codes for In-Person & Remote Interviews

Appearance matters to pretty much every employer, so make it count.

- **Remote interviews:** Even for video calls, reference the visual hygiene section in Chapter 3 and make sure you're camera-ready. Shoot for a clean and uncluttered background. Piles of dirty laundry aren't appealing to interviewers. Good lighting and a quiet space also make a big difference. And you've seen the video interview fails, so wear pants.

- **In-person:** Aim for business casual unless you know the company's dress code leans more formal. It's usually better to be slightly overdressed than too casual. This is also where the scent part of the hygiene section is extra important... be sure to remember your deodorant and suck on a mint right before you go in to interview.

Common Interview Questions & STAR Method

This is when those prepared stories come in handy. Behavioral questions are super common and generally start with, "Tell me about a time when..." They're meant to see how you handle situations, and the STAR method is used a bunch to answer them:

- **S (Situation):** Set the scene for your example. Briefly explain the context.

- **T (Task):** Describe what needed to be done or what the goal was.

- **A (Action):** Explain what you did to handle the situation.

- **R (Result):** Talk about the outcome and any positive impact you had.

Example Questions:

- "Tell me about a time you faced a challenge at work."

- "Describe a project where you had to work with a team."

- "How do you handle stressful situations?"

Following Up

A quick follow-up email can make them choose you over someone else. Within 24 hours, send a thank-you email just to say you appreciate their time and reiterate your interest in the job. Keep it short, polite, and specific. This is a pretty basic template, so you'll clearly want to change the wording to match how you sound. Otherwise, they'll assume you had AI write it, or you just copied something from online. There's nothing wrong with using AI or templates as a starting point, but it still has to sound like the genuine you.

Example Thank-You Email:

Subject: Thank You for the Interview

Hi [Interviewer's Name],

Thank you for the opportunity to discuss the [Job Title] position with you. I enjoyed learning more about [specific detail about the company or role] and am excited about the possibility of bringing my skills in [relevant skill or area] to your team. Please let me know if there's any additional information I can provide. Thanks again, and I look forward to hearing from you!

Best, [Your Name]

Workplace Dynamics

Knowing Generational Difference

Different age groups are absolutely going to have different communication styles and work preferences. You don't necessarily have to conform to their way of doing things, but understanding where they come from will help you navigate workplace culture. A good example is dress code expectations: If you show up for an interview dressed like you're going to a concert, older generations will probably dismiss you as being disrespectful.

Workplace Etiquette

Basics like clear email communication, professional behavior, and respecting the general workplace norms go a long way. This one's fairly simple. Don't gossip or eat someone's lunch, and things should be okay.

Constructive Criticism

Most of the time, feedback is a learning opportunity, even if it's hard to hear. There will obviously be times when someone is taking out their frustration on you, or they're just a bad leader. Outside of those occasions, constructive criticism can only help you get better.

Professional Boundaries

Another reminder that there's a difference between sharing and oversharing. Respect your coworkers' space and remember that remote work setups also require clear boundaries. If your work hours are 9 AM to 6 PM, then you shouldn't be expected to respond to messages at 8:30 PM.

Remote & Hybrid Work

Productive Workspace

Do your best with what you have to set up a comfortable, distraction-free area dedicated to work. Especially if other people in your house need help knowing when you're "in work mode."

Time Management & Accountability

Calendars, to-do lists, and time-blocking—whatever helps you stay on track. Remote work requires extra self-discipline to meet deadlines. You can only use so many excuses so many times.

Communication Tools & Etiquette

You likely already know Zoom, Slack, Asana, and all the other remote work tools. What really matters here is clear, concise communication—tone can easily be misinterpreted over just text.

Work-Life Boundaries

It's harder to set boundaries when your office is also your living room. Define your work hours and stick to them. Turn off notifications from work when you're done for the day.

Growth & Development

New Skills

Keep an eye out for online courses, certifications, and industry skills that can help you move forward. The more you know, the more you can make.

Mentors

This is a nice bonus of networking. Mentors can get you through tough job search processes or even set you up with interviews. If you find a good mentor, try to stick with them.

Career Goals

Work on setting realistic short- and long-term goals. Take it a step further with a step-by-step action plan so you can check in on your progress. It helps more than you'd think.

Advocate for Yourself

Know your worth. Don't be afraid to ask for raises, promotions, or new opportunities. It might not always have the results you want, but you miss one hundred percent of the shots you don't take.

Chapter 10:

Lists

New Home Necessities

It's the worst when you move in and realize you're missing about 20 essential things to live your life like a normal human. Best to avoid that if possible.

Linen Must-Haves:

- Bed sheets (at least two sets)
- Pillowcases
- Bath & hand towels
- Washcloths
- Blankets
- Kitchen towels

Kitchen Utensils:

- Spatula
- Large spoon (wooden or silicone)
- Tongs

- Knife set
- Can opener
- Measuring cups and spoons
- Cutting board

Bathroom Essentials:

- Toilet paper
- Shower curtain and hooks
- Hand soap
- Plunger
- Bathmat
- Trash can
- Toothbrush holder

Cleaning Supply Basics:

- All-purpose cleaner
- Dish soap and sponge
- Broom and dustpan
- Toilet brush
- Paper towels
- Laundry detergent
- Disinfecting wipes

Pantry Dry Goods:

- Rice
- Pasta
- Canned beans
- Flour
- Sugar
- Cooking oil
- Salt and pepper

Fridge Staples:

- Milk or dairy substitute
- Eggs
- Butter or margarine
- Fresh vegetables (like carrots, lettuce, or onions)
- Fruit (like apples or oranges)
- Cheese
- Condiments (ketchup, mustard, etc.)

First Aid:

- Band-aids
- Antiseptic wipes or cream
- Pain relievers (like ibuprofen)

- Thermometer
- Tweezers
- Gauze and tape

Tool Kit:

- Hammer
- Screwdriver set
- Pliers
- Measuring tape
- Utility knife
- Flashlight
- Duct tape

Chores

It takes less time to break up chores into smaller chunks than wait until everything piles up at once. Plus, there's less of an ick factor.

Daily:

- Make your bed
- Wash dishes
- Wipe down kitchen counters
- Wipe bathroom counters

- Tidy up common areas

Weekly:

- Vacuum or mop floors
- Clean bathroom surfaces and mirrors
- Dust furniture
- Do laundry
- Change bed linens
- Empty trash cans
- Wipe down kitchen appliances

Monthly:

- Clean inside the fridge
- Wipe down baseboards
- Dust ceiling fans and light fixtures
- Clean inside the microwave
- Wash windows
- Check and restock pantry staples
- Vacuum furniture

Twice a Year:

- Deep clean carpets or rugs
- Clean oven

- Declutter closets and drawers
- Wash pillows and comforters
- Check and replace smoke detector batteries
- Dust air vents
- Organize paperwork and shred unneeded documents

Once a Year:

- Clean behind and under major appliances
- Check expiration dates on pantry items
- Deep clean and reorganize storage areas
- Purge old clothes and donate
- Flip or rotate mattresses
- Replace air filters
- Clean gutters (if applicable)

Important Documents

Keep these all in the same place—drawer, folder, or even a fireproof safe:

- Birth certificate
- Social Security card
- Passport

- Health insurance card and details
- Lease or home ownership papers
- Car registration and insurance documents
- Medical information

Preparedness

Just a refresher on the emergency preparedness basics. For the contact list, phones and computers can die, so write things down somewhere as a backup.

Go-Bag Essentials:

- Water bottle
- Snacks (like granola bars)
- Flashlight and batteries
- Multi-tool or pocketknife
- First aid kit
- Phone charger and battery pack
- Extra clothes and personal hygiene items

Car Kit:

- Jumper cables
- Spare tire and jack

- First aid kit
- Blanket
- Non-perishable snacks and water
- Emergency phone charger
- Basic tool kit (screwdriver, wrench, etc.)

Emergency Contact List:

- Family members or close friends
- Primary care doctor
- Local hospital or urgent care
- Landlord or property manager
- Car insurance provider
- Poison control center (1-800-222-1222 in the U.S.)
- Workplace or school contact

The Go-To for Lists & Templates

There are tons more helpful things, like budget trackers, meal-planning charts, and to-do lists, if you really want to dive into the organization. But trying to stuff all of that into one chapter felt too intense, which is why I created a separate workbook. It's packed with ready-made templates and examples to simplify the essentials so you can focus on what matters most—building an amazing life!

Stay a step ahead of adulting and look for the *Adulting and Life Skills Workbook* on Amazon.

Conclusion

First things first: you just read a boatload of information, and it's okay not to have everything figured out. Adulting is a process, and no one expects you to master it overnight (or even in a few years). Everyone has felt unsure, messed up, and learned the hard way at least a dozen times. Life is messy and unpredictable, but that's part of what makes it amazing. The goal is progress, not perfection. If you're still learning, cool—everyone else is, too.

Let's do a quick recap just for fun:

- You can't get your time back, but you can make it work for you. Manage it well.

- Don't underestimate the power of small skills—knowing how to unclog a drain or cook a simple meal can save you money, time, and stress. A clean home is a relaxing home.

- Having a home you love, whether rented or owned, is one of the most satisfying parts of adult life, so it's good that you can manage utilities and keep your environment from falling apart.

- Regular checkups, exercise, and balanced eating are the best ways to feel good long-term. And let's be real: your future self will thank you for building these habits now.

- Whether you're saving for a big goal, paying down debt, or just learning to live within your means, basic budgeting and credit knowledge will set you up for success.

- Be ready for unexpected situations, from first aid to natural disasters. Knowing what to do in an emergency makes a big difference when it matters most.

- Filing taxes and knowing your rights isn't glamorous, but it is kind of empowering—and doing it right means fewer headaches later.

- Understanding options, safety, and travel etiquette make getting around easier and hopefully less dangerous.

- Remember the importance of speaking up and setting your personal limits.

- Resumes, interviews, workplace dynamics—no matter where your career takes you, you've got the know-how for getting there.

Now, let's talk about the fun stuff. Being an adult comes with a lot of perks—freedom, independence, and living life on your own terms in general. There's nothing better than deciding for yourself what you want your life to look like. You get to choose where to live, what to eat, who to spend time with, and how you make a living. You can travel on a whim, set your own rules, and make a space that feels completely yours.

Every small achievement matters. Even the boring ones. Maybe you made pancakes without burning them, figured out how to read a W2, or handled an awkward conversation at work really well—those are all wins. Each step you take in building your life is one more piece of the person you're becoming. Sure, some days will feel overwhelming. Bills, taxes, and responsibility aren't always fun. Most of the time, they make you want to stay in bed all day. But all those things are worth it.

Enjoy the little things, cut yourself some slack, and celebrate the progress you're making. It's a wild ride—it might actually try to kick you off now and then—but it's yours.

Have fun. Be safe. Live fully.

About the Author

Elizabeth Weston is a mother and grandmother with a Master's Degree in Education and National Board Teacher certification. Her work is targeted towards young adults and is designed to equip them with the knowledge and resources to handle much of the necessary business of life, the curveballs it throws along the way, as well as the critical skills and habits that will lay a strong foundation for their adult paths.

Elizabeth remembers her own experiences in her first years living independently from her parents and the mistakes made along the way because she did not know of or understand many of the tasks and responsibilities that adults are expected to handle, such as the importance of a credit score and how to build it, the assessing of personal property and, and much more. As time went by she remembers how much more efficiently things ran as she learned and applied organizational and management skills to her personal and work life. When her own children grew up and left the nest, she recalls many phone calls from them with questions on adult skills from how to sort the laundry, to how to apply for a passport. She funneled these experiences into the research for this book.

When she is not busy writing and researching, Elizabeth enjoys reading, spending time with her family, and traveling all over the world with her husband.

References

Agarwal, P. (2024, March 20). *8 Healthy Habits for Teens That Are Easy to Follow - Hola Health*. Hola Health | Online Doctor Consultation. https://hola.health/health-info/diet-lifestyle/8-healthy-habits-for-teens-that-are-easy-to-follow/

Bailey, J. (2021, February 28). *Teaching Your Teen the Basics of Auto Maintenance*. 2 Dads with Baggage. https://2dadswithbaggage.com/teaching-your-teen-the-basics-of-auto-maintenance/

Burgoyne, J. (2022, May 11). *Tips for Teaching Kids about Public Transport - Troomi Wireless*. Troomi Wireless. https://troomi.com/tips-for-teaching-kids-about-public-transport/

Care Health Insurance. (2024, May 22). *What Is the Need for Best Health Insurance for Teens?* Care Health Insurance. https://www.careinsurance.com/blog/health-insurance-articles/why-do-teenagers-need-health-insurance

Cleeve, L. (2019, February 25). *Public Transport Tips for Teens | RACV*. @RACV. https://www.racv.com.au/royalauto/transport/teens-public-transport.html

Domantas Vanagas. (2021, November 2). *Time Management for Teenagers | Personal Pivots*. Personal Pivots. https://personalpivots.com/time-management-tips-teenagers/

Flais, S. (2019). *Household Chores for Adolescents*. HealthyChildren.org. https://www.healthychildren.org/English/family-life/family-dynamics/Pages/Household-Chores-for-Adolescents.aspx

Georgia, D. S., & Kass, J. (2017, March 28). *Car Maintenance 101 for Teen Drivers*. Drive Smart Georgia. https://drivesmartgeorgia.com/blog/car-maintenance-101-teen-drivers/

GoHenry. (2023, January 9). *Budgeting for teens: a Guide for Parents and Teenagers*. Gohenry.com; GoHenry. https://www.gohenry.com/uk/blog/financial-education/how-to-teach-your-teenager-about-budgeting

GoHenry. (2024, March 13). *The Top 21 Chores for Teens to Level up Their Life Skills*. Gohenry.com; GoHenry. https://www.gohenry.com/uk/blog/chores/the-best-chores-for-teens

Health Insurance Basics (for Teens) - Nemours Kidshealth. (n.d.). Kidshealth.org. https://kidshealth.org/en/teens/insurance.html

Healthy Habits for Teens and How to Encourage Them. (2017, June 15). Orthodontics Limited. https://www.orthodonticslimited.com/your-health/healthy-habits-for-teens/

Heidi. (2017, April 22). *Life Skills as High School Electives: Basic Household Repairs for Teens*. StartsAtEight. https://www.startsateight.com/basic-household-repairs/

Lake, R. (2023, March 3). *Teens and Income Taxes*. Investopedia. https://www.investopedia.com/teens-and-income-taxes-7152618

Langston, G. (2023, January 27). *Healthy Habits Every Teen Should Embrace*. College Flight Plan. https://collegeflightplan.com/50-healthy-habits-your-teen-should-embrace/

McCullough, B. (1991). *Totally organized: Easy-to-use techniques for getting control of your time and your home*. St. Martin's Press.

Office of Population Affairs. (2022). *Healthy Relationships in Adolescence | HHS Office of Population Affairs*. Opa.hhs.gov. https://opa.hhs.gov/adolescent-health/healthy-relationships-adolescence

Peterson, R. (2018, May). *4 Time Robbers That Are Wrecking Your Progress*. Zandax.com; ZandaX. https://www.zandax.com/blog/4-time-robbers-that-are-wrecking-your-progress

Ponder, M. (2024, February 14). *Tax Basics for Teens: Filing Your First Tax Return*. TaxAct Blog. https://blog.taxact.com/taxes-for-teens-filing-your-first-tax-return/

Robertson, L. M., & Middleman, A. B. (1998). Knowledge of Health Insurance Coverage by Adolescents and Young Adults Attending a hospital-based Clinic. *Journal of Adolescent Health*, *22*(6), 439–445. https://doi.org/10.1016/s1054-139x(97)00270-x

Sippl, A. (2022, April 21). *What Safety Skills Does Your Teen Need to Know? | Life Skills Advocate*. Lifeskillsadvocate.com. https://lifeskillsadvocate.com/blog/what-safety-skills-does-your-teen-need-to-know/

Taxslayer Editorial Team. (2021, January 3). *Taxes for Teens - a Beginner's Guide*. The Official Blog of TaxSlayer. https://www.taxslayer.com/blog/teen-filing-first-tax-return/

Teens, B. on T. (2020, January 20). *How to Build Effective Relationships as a Teenager*. Back on Track Teens. https://www.backontrackteens.com/blog/build-effective-relationships-as-teenager/

Thrive Training and Consulting. (2021, November 11). *Tips for Teens: Building Healthy Communication Skills*. Thrive Training Consulting. https://www.thrivetrainingconsulting.com/tips-for-teens-building-healthy-communication-skills/

Wong, D. (2024, April 8). *Communication Skills for Teens: 7 Skills Every Teen Should Develop - Daniel Wong.* Daniel Wong. https://www.daniel-wong.com/2024/04/08/communication-skills-for-teens/

Made in United States
Troutdale, OR
02/25/2025